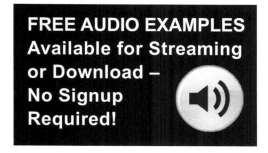

FREE AUDIO EXAMPLES Available for Streaming or Download – No Signup Required!

HOW TO |

Daily Lessons for Absolu

By Tristan Scroggins

MW01129976

All Photos of Tristan by Kaitlyn Raitz

ISBN: 9798543037324

HOW TO GET THE AUDIO

The audio files for this book are available for free as downloads or streaming on *troynelsonmusic.com*.

We are available to help you with your audio downloads and any other questions you may have. Simply email *help@troynelsonmusic.com*.

See below for the recommended ways to listen to the audio:

Download Audio Files (Zipped)	Stream Audio Files
• Download Audio Files (Zipped)	• Recommended for CELL PHONES & TABLETS
• Recommended for COMPUTERS on WiFi	• Bookmark this page
• A ZIP file will automatically download to the default "downloads" folder on your computer	• Simply tap the PLAY button on the track you want to listen to
• Recommended: download to a desktop/laptop computer *first*, then transfer to a tablet or cell phone	• Files also available for streaming or download at *soundcloud.com/troynelsonbooks*
• Phones & tablets may need an "unzipping" app such as iZip, Unrar or Winzip	
• Download on WiFi for faster download speeds	

To download the companion audio files for this book, visit: troynelsonmusic.com/audio-downloads/

INTRODUCTION

Congrats on buying this book and taking your first steps towards becoming a mandolin player! Whether you want to play tunes for friends and family, perform on stage, or simply play privately for your own enjoyment, music can add so much enrichment to our lives, and the mandolin is a really great instrument to do that with. It's small size and limited number of strings make it very accessible and easy to start on, but it has the potential to be played in many different types of music, including bluegrass, classical, blues, Brazilian choro, jazz, folk, and many more.

The mandolin is an Italian instrument that is related to the lute. Older versions of the instrument had a small teardrop-shaped flat top, with a round bowl-shaped back. These are sometimes referred to as "taterbug" mandolins. Around the turn of the 20th century, Orville Gibson, a luthier living in Kalamazoo, Michigan, invented a new style of mandolin that had a carved top and back, F-shaped soundholes, a raised fingerboard, and an ornamental shape. This would eventually morph into what we now call an F-style mandolin, and Gibson Mandolin-Guitar Mfg. Co. Ltd. would go on to make some of the most famous guitars in the world. Today, there are many different shapes and styles of mandolin—and just as many different types of music you can hear the mandolin in.

This book will mostly be taught through the lens of bluegrass mandolin because that's what I specialize in. However, even if you don't plan on playing bluegrass, the techniques taught in this book will lay a solid foundation for whatever style you hope to play. I started playing mandolin when I was 9 years old. I had grown up hearing music because my dad is a National Banjo Champion and his grandfather was a National Fiddle Champion. My dad didn't play the mandolin, so I bought a method book (not dissimilar to this one) and a friend of ours would drive down to give me lessons once a week and then call me on the phone every night to make sure I was practicing. His name was Bob Fisher and, in addition to teaching me how to play the mandolin, he passed on a great passion for teaching. I'm thankful for the guidance of both my father and Bob and all the numerous teachers and mentors I've had along the way. I'm so excited and honored to get to pass on this tradition to you, as well.

This book is dedicated to Jeff Scroggins, Bob Fisher, and Megan Lynch, with special thanks to Bethany Olds.

HOW TO USE THIS BOOK

How to Play Mandolin in 14 Days is divided into 14 lessons, one for each day of the two-week program. Within each lesson/day are six "mini-lessons." The goal is to spend 15 minutes practicing the music exercise(s) in each mini-lesson, for a total of 90 minutes (15 X 6 = 90) per day. The two exceptions are Day 7 and Day 14. On these days, the entire 90 minutes are devoted to a single song that reviews the material presented during the previous six days.

Granted, 90 minutes of practice per day can seem daunting to some, especially if you are unaccustomed to practice sessions lasting longer than 20–30 minutes. And that's OK! Just because the book is structured to teach you mandolin in 14 days doesn't mean you have to follow the program precisely. On the contrary, if you have, say, 30 minutes to devote to the book each day, then simply extend each section to a three-day practice session. The material is there for you to use, whether you get through the book in 14 days or 40.

While the 14-day plan is the goal, it's probably unrealistic for some. The important thing is to stick with it, because the material in this book will have you playing the mandolin with confidence and credibility. How quickly just depends on the amount of time you're able to spend on getting there.

Before you begin your daily sessions, however, I suggest spending at least 15–20 minutes listening to the accompanying audio to get a feel for the forthcoming exercises, as well as reading the text in each section for some pointers and to better understand the material you're about to learn. That way, you can spend the full 90 minutes (or however much time you have to practice that day) practicing the actual exercises.

To help you keep track of time in your practice sessions, time codes are included throughout the book. Simply set the timer on your smart phone to 90 minutes (1:30)—or however much time you can dedicate to your session—and move on to a new section every 15 minutes. Or you can set the timer to 15 minutes (0:15) and move on to the next category when the timer goes off.

Next, set your metronome (or click track) to a tempo at which you can play the exercise all the way through without making too many mistakes (40–50 beats per minute is probably a good starting point for most exercises). Once you're able to play the exercise cleanly, increase your tempo by 2–5 BPM. Again, make sure you can play through the exercise without making too many mistakes. If the speed is too fast, back off a bit until your execution is precise. Continue to increase your tempo incrementally until it's time to move on to the next section.

There will be times when the timer goes off but you feel like you didn't adequately learn the material. When this happens, I suggest moving on to the next section, nonetheless. It may seem counterintuitive, but it's better to continue progressing through the book than to prolong the practice session while trying to perfect the material. After you've completed the book, you can always go back and review the exercises. In fact, I recommend it. Making steady progress, while not always perfectly, keeps you mentally sharp and motivated. Focusing too much on any one exercise is a sure way to sidetrack your sessions.

Lastly—and this is important—if you ever feel yourself getting physically fatigued, or pain develops in any part of your body, immediately take a break until the discomfort subsides, whether it's for 10 minutes, an hour, or for the rest of the day. You never want to push yourself beyond your physical limits and cause permanent damage. As mentioned earlier, the material isn't going anywhere; you can always go back to it when you're feeling 100%.

GETTING STARTED

Before we jump into playing the mandolin, we have to know how to hold it. It's important to practice with healthy and intentional technique. The two main reasons are: 1) proper technique is meant to maximize our efficiency on the instrument, and if we slack on technique, we're only making the learning process harder on ourselves, and 2) proper technique keeps us from injuring ourselves. Playing an instrument requires a lot of repetitive motion, and playing improperly can lead to back, shoulder, elbow, and wrist problems. We want to make sure we have a long, healthy relationship with our instrument.

Motivating ourselves to learn proper technique can be hard when we want to get right to playing music but remember: practice doesn't make perfect. *Perfect* practice makes perfect.

Your Instrument

It doesn't matter what type of mandolin you have, as long as it has eight strings, you'll be able to use this book (although some of it might not sound as good on a bowlback mandolin). However, there are some things that will make the instrument a little easier or harder to play.

There are two main styles of mandolin: A-style and F-style. A-style mandolins have a body that is shaped like a teardrop, and F-style mandolins have a body with two points on one side and a scroll on the other. Both styles will usually have a button on the bottom of the body (below where the strings end). This is used for one end of a strap. Straps are useful, especially for A-styles, when it comes to keeping the instrument upright.

A-style Mandolin

F-style Mandolin

If you have an F-style, you can just thread the other end of the strap through the scroll. With an A-style, we have to get a little more creative. There *might* be another button on the back of the mandolin, where the neck meets the body, which you can attach the strap to. Most likely, you'll have to attach it to the headstock (the part with the tuning pegs). To do this, take a piece of string (strong string, like twine, not thread) and thread it between the headstock and the strings, just behind the nut (the white plastic-like material at the beginning of the fretboard). Tie the ends of the string together so you have a small loop attached to the headstock. Now attach your strap to this loop. (If you have a bowlback mandolin, a quick Google search can quickly find tips for adding a strap.)

The other variable is your bridge. Most modern mandolins have an adjustable bridge, which can be identified by the little metal wheels on its sides. Some mandolins have a solid-piece bridge that cannot be adjusted. Either way, I do not recommend adjusting the bridge yourself. When you first get your mandolin, and about once a year after that, you should take it to a professional to get set up. Think of it like changing the oil in your car. Try to take it to a music shop that specializes in *acoustic* instruments and ask them to set it up for you. They'll adjust the bridge and neck (if they're adjustable), which will allow the instrument to play in tune, as well as make it easier to play.

Tuning

The mandolin has eight total strings but they are tuned in pairs; in other words, each pitch is doubled. The tuning is the same as the violin. Starting with the lowest string (the thickest one and closest to your head), the pitches are as follows: **G–D–A–E**. But, like I said, the strings are tuned in pairs, so the tuning would actually be **GG–DD–AA–EE**. To save time and headache, we often refer to the pairs of strings as just one string. In this book, I might refer to the "D string" but mean the *two* D strings. And, occasionally, I will refer to the pairs of strings as "courses."

◀)) TUNING NOTES: G–D–A–E

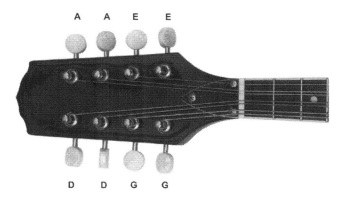

When tuning the mandolin, it is really easy to accidentally turn the wrong tuning peg and then break a string. Just be careful that you're turning the *correct* knob. When tuning, it's best to tune up to a note. In other words, if we're tuning the G string and notice that it's a little sharp, rather than tuning down until we reach G, it is better to tune until we are a little flat and then tune *up* to G. This just keeps the note from slipping while we're playing.

Left Hand – Holding the Instrument

When holding the neck of the instrument in your left hand, it's important to remember not to "choke the chicken." This means that you don't want to wrap your whole hand around it. Rather, you should rest the neck on the first joint, or knuckle, of your index finger, right around the first fret. Then place the joint of your thumb around the same place but on the other side of the neck. This should leave a gap between the back of the neck and your hand. Unlike on the guitar or bass, we will not be placing our thumb behind the neck to get the leverage we need to push down on the strings. Instead, these two points of contact on the sides of the neck will work together to allow us to use our fingertips.

When pressing on a string, you only want to use the tip of your finger—you'll almost never use the pads of your fingers and very rarely would a finger ever lay flat across the strings. Try to always approach a string from above by creating arches with your fingers. This will allow you to play individual notes without accidentally muting other strings. When fretting the instrument, make sure that your finger is just behind the desired fret, not on top of it.

Always keep your wrist straight and relaxed. If you find yourself wanting to adjust your wrist, try moving your elbow closer to or further from your body. This will cause your hand to rotate on the axis of your index finger and can give you the extra room you may need to make a particular chord.

In this book, I will refer to the fingers as the index, middle, ring, and pinky. In the music examples, these fingers will be notated as 1, 2, 3, and 4:

Index = 1
Middle = 2
Ring = 3
Pinky = 4

Right Hand – Holding the Pick

There are lots of different ways to hold a pick. People have a lot of opinions about this but I've never believed that there is only one right way. In fact, my pick moves around a lot while I'm playing because the pick's position changes the timbre of the notes being played and, with practice, that can be used purposefully for effect.

Let's start with the pick. Chances are, you're currently holding a guitar pick. Guitar picks are teardrop-shaped and usually fairly thin and made of plastic. Using guitar picks on the mandolin is perfectly acceptable; however, most bluegrass musicians use a slightly different style of pick. Mandolin picks are usually closer to being an equilateral triangle with rounded edges. They are usually thick, meaning they don't bend easily, and often made of plastic, but many players opt for harder materials, so you will see picks made out of various synthetic materials or tortoise shells. These picks help create a loud, full, crisp sound that is important to that style of music. Other genres, such as traditional Irish or Brazilian choro, opt for different shapes and thicknesses of picks.

I'll explain the most standard pick grip. Start with a loose fist, with your thumb on the outside. We're going to place the pick between the thumb and the side of your curled index finger. Make sure that your thumb is slightly flexed (in other words, if you're double-jointed, don't overextend your thumb). If you're using a teardrop-shaped pick, make sure the longest end is pointing outward. If you're using a mandolin pick, any side will work. If you think of your thumb as pointing in a direction, the pick should point in the direction that is perpendicular to the joint of the thumb. Keep this grip *loose*. This will take practice but you shouldn't feel like you're squeezing the pick.

You don't want too much or too little of the pick sticking out from your grip; you want it to stick out enough so that there's give when it comes in contact with the string but also inside the grip enough so that you have control of it.

Your arm should approach the bridge from an angle, not from behind it. The best practice is to avoid anchoring your right hand on the instrument. However, I anchored for many years and many players anchor and sound great. Ideally, your wrist will be slightly bent and floating over the strings. Some people anchor the palm of their hand on the side of the bridge (which mutes the sound and can potentially move the bridge), while others will plant their pinky finger on the body of the instrument (which slightly mutes the sound and limits the movement of the right hand). Both of these anchors can help control the movement of the right hand but simultaneously limit our movement (confusing, I know). Ideally, we'd be using just our wrist to move the pick when we play melodies and activating more of the arm muscles for rhythm playing. But, like I said, there are many roads to Rome.

A Brief Note on Music Theory

This book doesn't get heavily into music theory but occasionally it's unavoidable. That's because music theory is the language that we use to describe the sounds of music. While it can be useful to use theory to understand the relationships in music, it's complexity often creates barriers that can intimidate people. Additionally, in an attempt to combat the complexity, many styles of folk music have created colloquial versions of theory that specifically apply to their genre.

I don't think it's hugely important for you to understand music theory, or to even be able to read music, in order to learn how to play. However, I wanted to outline a couple of ideas that will be presented in this book.

In particular, I want to discuss using numbers to describe chords. *Chords* are combinations of three or more notes. When we are in a particular key, there are chords that we commonly use together. Let's look at how we find those chords.

In most Western music, there are 12 unique notes that we can play (some of them have two different names, depending on the context in which they're used):

C   C♯/D♭   D   D♯/E♭   E   F   F♯/G♭   G   G♯/A♭   A   A♯/B♭   B

Each one of these notes are a *semitone* (sometimes called a *half step*) apart. Two semitones equal one *whole tone* (sometimes called a *whole step*). We can create scales by using different combinations of these whole tones and semitones. In fact, we define scales by the pattern of intervals (distance between notes) we use to create the scales.

The pattern for a major scale is *whole–whole–half–whole–whole–whole–half*. So, if we start with that C note, then go up a whole step, we get a D note. Go up another whole step and we get an E note. Then go up a half step and we get an F note, and so on. If you continued this pattern, you'd get the C major scale: C–D–E–F–G–A–B.

Now, for convenience's sake, let's number each of those notes, from 1 to 7:

C	D	E	F	G	A	B	C
1	2	3	4	5	6	7	1

To make a chord, we're going play the 1st, 3rd, and 5th notes—C, E, and G—together. This three-note chord, C major, is called a *triad*. If we harmonized each note of the C major scale, using this same pattern (i.e., every other note), we'd end up with this:

C	D	E	F	G	A	B	C
E	F	G	A	B	C	D	E
G	A	B	C	D	E	F	G

Now, if we named the chords, we would get the following ("m" denotes a minor chord, and "°" denotes a diminished chord):

C	Dm	Em	F	G	Am	B°	C

Then, if we numbered these chords, we'd get:

C	Dm	Em	F	G	Am	B°	C
1	2	3	4	5	6	7	1

Although we sometimes prefer to use Roman numerals when talking about chords because we can add more information. For example, if the numeral is capitalized, the chord is major; if it's lowercase, the chord is minor. Here's how that looks:

C	Dm	Em	F	G	Am	B°	C
1	2	3	4	5	6	7	1
I	ii	iii	IV	V	vi	vii°	I

The numbers denote a *relationship* to the tonic, or I chord, that is true no matter what key we are in. If we went through this same process but starting on the note A, we'd end up with:

A	Bm	C♯m	D	E	F♯m	G♯°	A

But we could still number the chords in the same way:

A	Bm	C♯m	D	E	F♯m	G♯°	A
1	2	3	4	5	6	7	1
I	ii	iii	IV	V	vi	vii°	I

This is important because most songs you're going to play will only use the I, IV, and V chord. So, in a jam, you can say, "This is a 1–4–5 song in the key of D," instead of having to say, "This song is in the key of D and it uses the D major, G major, and A major chords." It's a bit of shorthand that is useful and will become more obvious once we start playing.

PARTS OF THE MANDOLIN

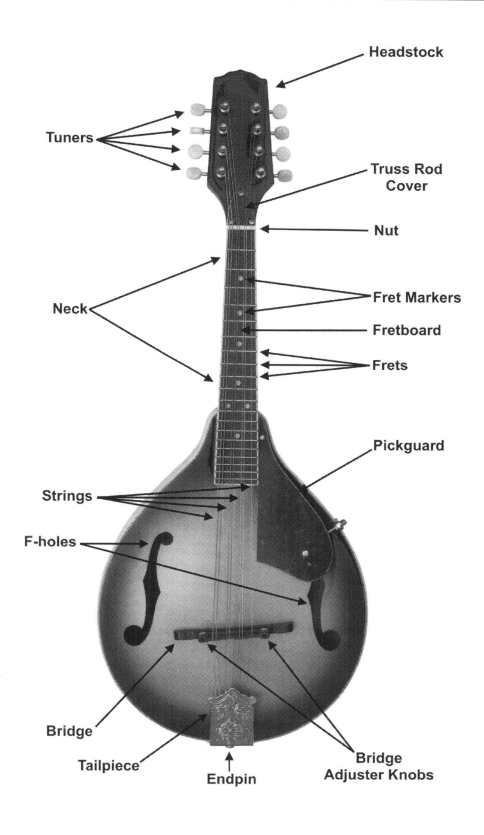

Headstock

Tuners

Truss Rod Cover

Nut

Neck

Fret Markers

Fretboard

Frets

Pickguard

Strings

F-holes

Bridge

Tailpiece

Endpin

Bridge Adjuster Knobs

CHORD DIAGRAMS & TAB

The music examples in this book are presented in a couple of different formats: chord diagrams and rhythm tab. In this section, we're going to go over each format so you'll be able to quickly apply the music to your instrument as you go through the book. Let's start with chord diagrams.

Chord Diagrams

A *chord diagram*, or *chord frame*, is simply a graphical representation of a small section (usually four or five frets) of the mandolin neck, or fretboard. Vertical lines represent the mandolin's four strings, horizontal lines represent frets, and black dots indicate where your fingers should be placed. Although a bit counterintuitive, chord diagrams are presented as though you're looking at the neck while the guitar is held vertically in front of you rather than from a more natural horizontal position. Nevertheless, chord frames are a good way to quickly understand how a chord should be "voiced," or fingered.

A thick, black horizontal line at the top of the diagram indicates the mandolin's nut (the plastic-like string-spacer at the end of the fretboard). When this is present, the chord typically incorporates one or more open strings, which are represented by hollow circles above the frame. Conversely, when a string is not to be played, an "X" will appear above the frame.

When more than one note is fretted by the same finger, or "barred," a slur encompasses the notes (*barre chords* get their name from this technique). If a chord is played higher up the neck, above the 4th of 5th fret, the nut is replaced by a thin horizontal line and the fret number is indicated next to the lowest fret (highest in the diagram). Sometimes—but not always—the chord's fingering is included at the bottom of the frame: 1 = index, 2 = middle, 3 = ring, and 4 = pinky.

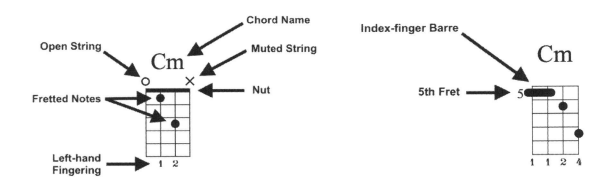

Tab

A tab staff looks much like a standard treble or bass clef; however, if you look a little closer, you'll notice that it contains *four* lines instead of five. Those four lines represent the four strings of the mandolin, with the G string positioned at the bottom, and the E string at the top. Tab contains no key signature because there are no notes to deal with; instead, numbers are placed on the strings to represent the frets of the mandolin neck. So, for example, if you see the number 2 on the G string, you would fret that string at fret 2. Or, if you see the number 0 stacked on the G and D strings, you would pick those strings together, open (unfretted).

Sometimes, you'll see tab accompanied by standard notation, and other times you'll see tab-only music (we'll be using the latter in this book). Tab-only music often includes rhythm symbols (stems, flags, beams, rests, etc.), as well. Rhythm symbols in tab are the same as those you'll find in standard notation but the noteheads are replaced by fret numbers. Because we incorporate rhythm, the tab includes a time signature and requires a fundamental understanding of rhythm, which you can learn more about in the Breakdown of Rhythms section (unlike standard notation, however, we don't have to worry about key signatures).

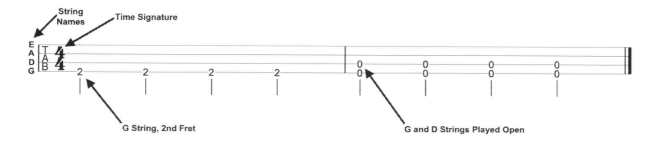

CHORD CHART

OPEN CHORDS

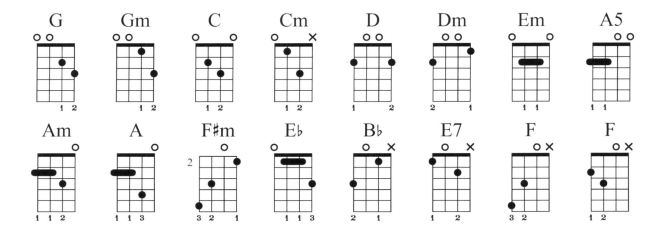

CLOSED CHORDS

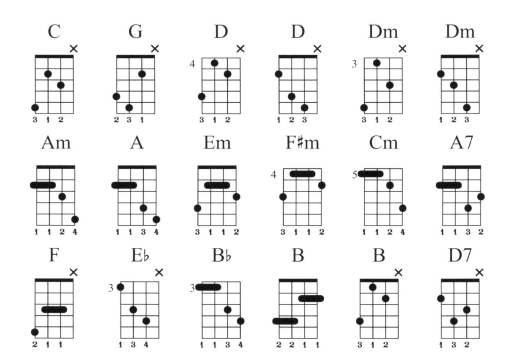

BREAKDOWN OF RHYTHMS

Circles, stems, beams, and flags are written on the lines and spaces of a music or tab staff to indicate rhythm. Also included on the staff are *bar lines,* which are perpendicular lines drawn in increments. The space between these bar lines is called a *measure,* or *bar.*

At the beginning of the staff, you'll see the *time signature.* The most common time signature is 4/4 ("four-four") time, which indicates that each measure contains four beats (top number), and a quarter note is equal to one beat (bottom number).

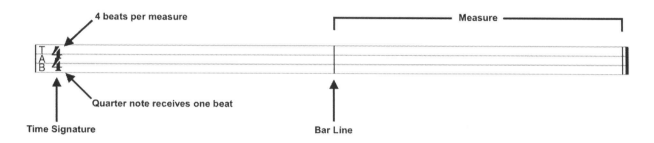

The following is a breakdown of the rhythms that you'll encounter as you go through the book.

A *whole note* has a rhythmic value of four beats, or an entire measure in 4/4 time (i.e., a four-beat measure). Here is what one whole note looks like:

A *whole rest* indicates four beats of silence, or an entire measure in 4/4 time. Here is what one whole rest looks like:

A *half note* has a rhythmic value of two beats, or half of a measure in 4/4 time. Here is what one measure of half notes looks like:

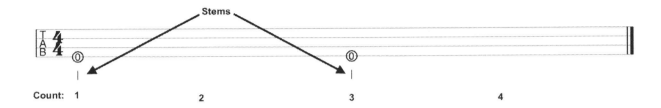

A *half rest* indicates two beats of silence, or half of a measure in 4/4 time. A half rest has the same rhythmic value as a half note:

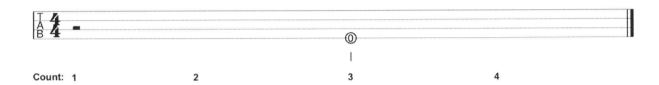

A *quarter note* has a rhythmic value of one beat, or 1/4 of a measure in 4/4 time. Here is what one measure of quarter notes looks like:

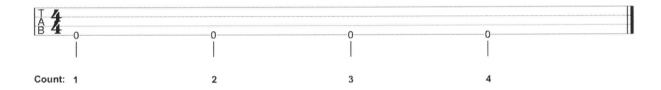

A *quarter rest* indicates one beat of silence, or 1/4 of a measure in 4/4 time. A quarter rest has the same rhythmic value as a quarter note:

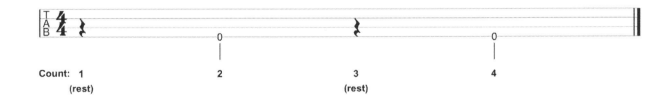

An *eighth note* has a rhythmic value of half a beat, or 1/8 of a measure in 4/4 time. Here is what one measure of eighth notes looks like:

Beamed Eighth Notes

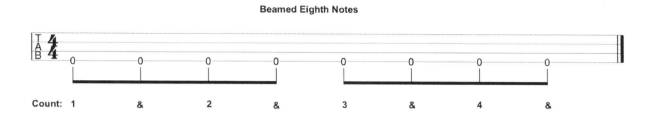

An *eighth rest* indicates a half beat of silence, or 1/8 of a measure in 4/4 time. An eighth rest has the same rhythmic value as an eighth note:

Flagged Eighth Notes

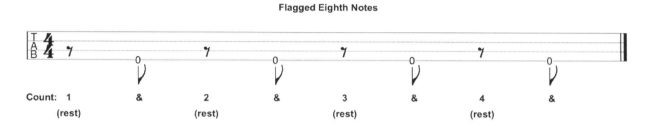

An *eighth-note triplet* consists of three eighth notes in a space (one beat) typically occupied by two eighth notes. Here is what one measure of eighth-note triplets looks like:

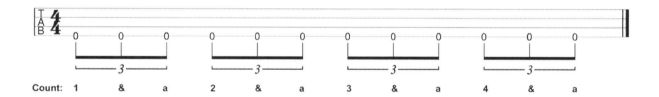

WEEK 1
DAY 1

RIGHT HAND: DOWNSTROKES (1:30–1:15) 🔊

Downstrokes are pretty easy because we have gravity to help us out. Draw the pick through both of the open strings in a downward motion, using your wrist. Then bring it back above the string and do it again. This can be done in quarter notes while counting "1, 2, 3, 4," etc. Beats that we count with numbers (i.e., strong beats) will almost always be plucked with downstrokes. Play four downstrokes on each string and repeat.

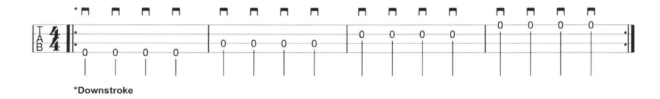

*Downstroke

LEFT HAND: HALF STEP WITH THE INDEX AND MIDDLE 🔊 FINGERS (1:15–1:00)

We change what notes we're playing by pressing down the strings with the fingers on our left hand. We press the strings down right behind (not on top of) the fret wire (but not so close that the meat of our finger goes beyond the middle of the fret). This changes the length of the string, causing it to vibrate at a higher pitch.

First position is the basic outline for which fingers we use to play which notes. First position means the index finger will play the 1st and 2nd frets, the middle finger will play the 3rd and 4th frets, the ring finger will play the 5th and 6th frets, and the pinky will occasionally play the 6th fret but always play the 7th fret.

Everything in Week 1 will be in 1st position, whereas Week 2 will touch on 3rd position. *Third position* means our first (index) finger will be playing the notes that the third (ring) finger usually plays in 1st position. We do this so we can play higher notes on the fretboard—and we use positions so we don't get lost!

Use your index finger to push down the G string at the 2nd fret and play a downstroke. Then use your middle finger to push down the G string at the 3rd fret and play another downstroke. Repeat this sequence once and then move on to the next string. You should be pushing down enough so that the note rings clear but not so hard that the string is bending over the fret. (Refer to the Getting Started section in the introduction to check your left-hand technique.) If you are new to stringed instruments, this may be slightly painful. Building up calluses on your fingers takes time, but you'll eventually develop the ability to press down gently and confidently with little effort.

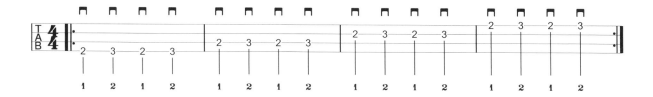

MAJOR CHORDS: G MAJOR (1:00–0:45) 🔊

Let's learn our first chord! *Chords* are three or more notes played at the same time. On the mandolin, that usually means we are using our left hand to push down multiple strings at once.

To make a G major chord, we're going to take our index finger and put it on the 2nd fret of the A string (this is a B note). Then, we're going to take our middle finger and place it on the 3rd fret of the E string (this is a G note). When we play these two notes along with the open G and D strings, we have a G major chord. Draw your pick down through all four courses of strings in one smooth motion. When playing chords, it's OK to use more of your arm. Try to keep your wrist loose and use your elbow to move your hand through the strings.

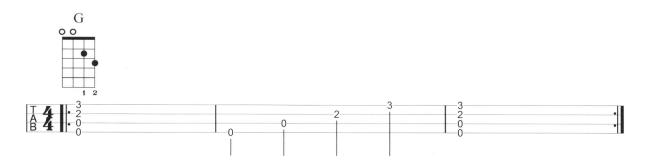

MINOR CHORDS: G MINOR (0:45–0:30) 🔊

People often explain the difference between major and minor chords by describing major as sounding "happy" and minor as sounding "sad" (though that is a bit of an oversimplification). To change a major chord to a minor chord, we often only need to move one finger back by one fret. In the case of G, to make it a minor chord, we place our index finger on the 1st fret of the A string while our middle finger remains on the 3rd fret of the E string. When we play these two notes along with the open G and D strings, we get a G minor chord.

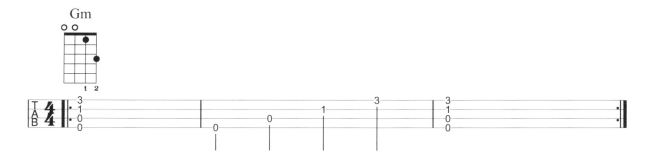

RHYTHM: BOOM CHUCK (0:30–0:15) 🔊

One of the most basic rhythms we can play on the mandolin is the "boom-chuck" rhythm. This is the rhythm that bluegrass guitarists use and it gets its name from the sound that the notes make when played on the guitar. We'll start by holding a G major chord. Then, on beats 1 and 3, we are going to use a downstroke to play a note on one of our low strings—in this case, the open G string. On beats 2 and 4, we're going to play all four strings by strumming the chord (also using a downstroke). All together it goes: 1) single string, 2) full chord strum, 3) single string, 4) full chord strum—or 1) "boom," 2) "chuck," 3) "boom," 4) "chuck."

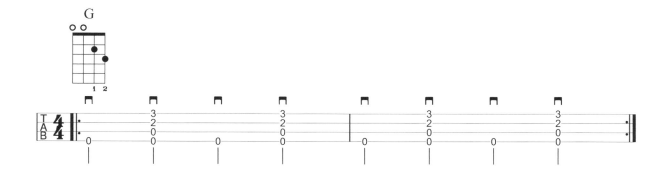

Below is a variation on the first example. This one alternates notes on the G and D strings.

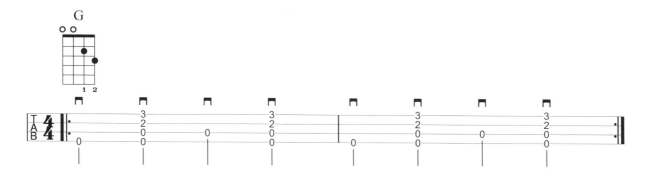

ORNAMENTS: UPWARD SLIDE (0:15–0:00) 🔊

Ornaments are little things we can do to spice up our playing. They often involve the left hand.

A *slide* is exactly what it sounds like: we are going to play a note and then, while the note is still ringing, slide the finger on our left hand to another fret. If done correctly, the note will finish ringing with the pitch of the new fret. We are going to start by sliding *up*, which means towards the bridge.

Start with your middle finger on the 3rd fret of the D string. Play this note as a downstroke and then, while the note is still ringing, slide your finger up to the 4th fret. Then stop pressing down and move your finger back to the 3rd fret to repeat. Try to count it as: 1) downstroke, 2) slide, 3) downstroke, 4) slide.

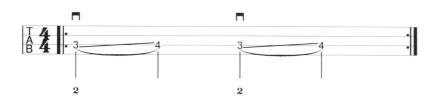

DAY 2

RIGHT HAND: UPSTROKES (1:30–1:15) 🔊

An *upstroke* involves pulling the pick up from under a course of strings; in other words, it's the opposite of a downstroke. We almost always play downstrokes on the beats we count with a number (1, 2, 3, 4), whereas upstrokes are almost always used on the beats in between those numbers, which we count with an "and" (1-**&**, 2-**&**, 3-**&**, 4-**&**).

Make sure that your pick goes through both strings. This motion can be awkward at first—and you might find yourself wanting to use the muscles in your forearm to move your arm and hand—but you want to try to mostly use your wrist, with your arm moving very little. The motion is a combination of moving your hand straight up and down with the wrist as the pivot point and a slight twisting motion in your forearm, similar to how you would turn a key in a lock. This will create a motion that allows the pick to brush the string like a paint brush.

Try playing four notes on each open string with an upstroke. To keep time, count aloud ("1-&, 2-&, 3-&, 4-&," etc.) and play an upstroke when you say "and."

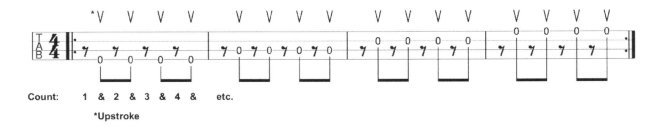

Count: 1 & 2 & 3 & 4 &   etc.

*Upstroke

LEFT HAND: WHOLE STEP WITH THE INDEX AND 🔊 MIDDLE FINGERS (1:15–1:00)

Let's practice using our index and middle fingers again. Yesterday, we played the 2nd and 3rd frets, but today we're going to play the 2nd and 4th frets of each string. In music, we describe the distance between notes in "steps." On the mandolin, the distance from one fret to the next is a *half step*, and the distance of two frets is a *whole step*. So, today, we're going to be practicing *whole* steps.

Start with your index finger on the 2nd fret of the G string and play a downstroke. Now place your middle finger on the 4th fret of the G string and play another downstroke. Go back to the second fret and play a downstroke, followed by the 4th fret with a downstroke. Now switch to the next string and do the same. Continue this pattern through all four strings.

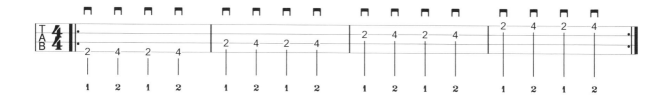

MAJOR CHORDS: C MAJOR (1:00–0:45) 🔊

The C major chord is very similar to the G major chord we just learned. You'll put your index and middle fingers on the same frets but this time on the two middle strings (D and A).

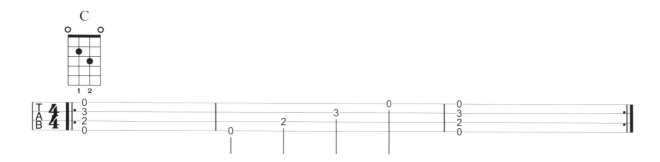

MINOR CHORDS: C MINOR (0:45–0:30) 🔊

Just like with the G minor chord, we can start with a C major chord and then move our index finger back by one fret to make it C *minor*. But there's one problem: the C major chord has our index finger on the 2nd fret of the D string, which is an E note. When we move it down to the 1st fret, this turns it into an E♭ note and transforms the chord from major to minor, except that our open E string is still playing an E note and will sound really bad against these other notes. In a couple of days, we'll learn a technique to fix this problem, but for now, experiment with trying to strum only the bottom three strings (G, D, and A) when you play this chord.

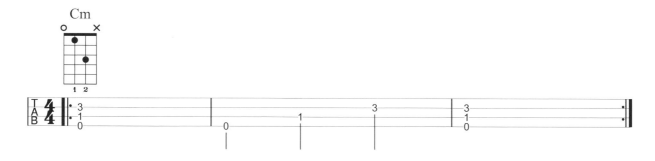

RHYTHM: FOLK STRUM PATTERN (0:30–0:15)

While the boom-chuck pattern is common in country and bluegrass, it can sometimes feel lacking if you're the only rhythm player. I always associate the strum pattern that we're about to learn with folk music. We'll be using the C major chord we just learned.

This pattern uses both downstrokes and upstrokes. Just like when playing lead, most beats counted with a number will be a downstroke through the strings, and most beats counted with an "and" will be an upstroke (although those rules are more likely to be broken while playing rhythm). So, a rhythm counted "1-&, 2-&, 3-&, 4-&" would be played down-up, down-up, down-up, down-up.

The rhythm below is counted "1, 2-&, (3)-&, 4-&," so the strums will be down, down-up, up, down-up (no strum occurs on beat 3 but it still should be counted). Before we play it on the mandolin, try clapping the rhythm while counting out loud. You'll say, "1-&, 2-&, 3-&, 4-&," while clapping on all the beats in bold: **1**-&, **2**-&, 3-**&**, **4**-**&**.

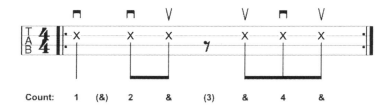

Once that feels comfortable, try it on the mandolin. Remember: when playing rhythm, we can use more of our arm muscles while keeping a loose wrist.

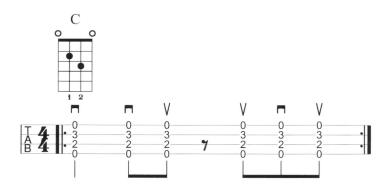

28

ORNAMENTS: HAMMER-ON (0:15–0:00) 🔊

A *hammer-on* is similar to a slide in that we are going to change the pitch of a note while it's still ringing by using our left hand. For this move, we will play a note and then use a different finger to play a higher fret, causing the pitch to go up. The trick is that, if you move too slow, your finger will stop the string from vibrating and you won't be able to hear the new note, so confidence is key.

Let's start by putting our index finger on the 2nd fret of the D string. Play the string with a downstroke and then use your middle finger to quickly push down the 4th fret of the D (same) string. When you're first getting started, you just need to make sure you're pushing down before the note stops ringing. You may feel the urge to lift your index finger up when you put the middle finger down, but that will only cause problems, so keep them both down! Once it feels comfortable, set your metronome to a comfortable tempo, and then try to time it so you play the first note on the numbered beats (1, 2, 3, 4) and perform the hammer-on on the "and" beats.

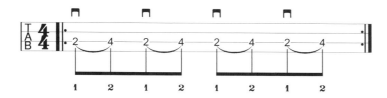

DAY 3

RIGHT HAND: EIGHTH NOTES (1:30–1:15) 🔊

In 4/4 time, a whole note gets four beats. A quarter note is played for 1/4 of a whole note, meaning we would play a quarter note (with a downstroke) on each of the numbered beats: 1, 2, 3, 4. Meanwhile, an eighth note is half as long as a quarter note (or twice as fast, depending on how you want to think of it). So, to count eighth notes in the space of a whole note (one measure), we count "1-&, 2-&, 3-&, 4-&."

Beats that we count with numbers are almost always played with downstrokes, and beats we count with "and" are almost always played with upstrokes. We touched on this in yesterday's folk strum, but now we're going to strum steady streams of uninterrupted eighth notes on each string. On the open G string, play a downstroke and count "1." Then play an upstroke and count it as "and." Then repeat that by playing a downstroke and counting "2," followed by an upstroke counted as "and," and so on. Then move to the next string and start on "1" again.

Try to pull through the string by using your wrist. It will take some time to get the up-and-down motion smooth (gravity helps with downstrokes, making them easier). You want to be able to play eighth notes with enough control that the downstrokes and upstrokes are indistinguishable. One of the biggest problems I see in intermediate-level players is their control (or lack thereof) over eighth notes. What ends up happening is that the first downstroke is in time but the subsequent upstroke is late because they struggle with upstrokes. Then they'll play the next downstroke too quickly to compensate, and the cycle continues. This truncates both the notes and their rhythm in a way that doesn't sound very musical. So, make sure you work on both downstrokes *and* upstrokes.

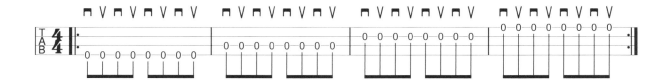

LEFT HAND: ADDING THE RING FINGER (1:15–1:00) 🔊

So far, we've only used our index and middle fingers, but let's try adding the ring finger to the little exercise below. We'll start on the G string. Use a downstroke and your index finger on the 2nd fret to play the first note, then an upstroke and your middle finger on the 4th fret to play the next. Now, with a downstroke, play the 5th fret with your *ring* finger. Let that note be twice as long as the first two notes. Then repeat this sequence on the D string, the A string, and the E string. The count should be "1-&, 2, 3-&, 4." When you're starting out, just try to get comfortable with using the ring finger. Then, when you're ready, set a metronome and try to play this exercise in time.

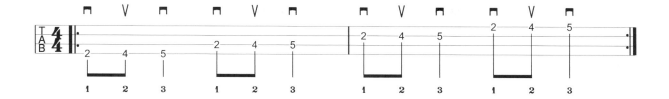

MAJOR CHORDS: D MAJOR (1:00–0:45) 🔊

This chord was taught to me as the "hippie D chord." What people meant was this chord was more useful in folk music than it was in bluegrass. The reason for this is that folk rhythm often involves more ringing chords, whereas bluegrass rhythm (on the mandolin) is often accented like a snare drum. This D chord uses open strings, so it naturally wants to ring more than be cut short (we'll discuss the differences in those rhythms soon).

For now, take your index finger and place it on the 2nd fret of the G string. Next, you're going to put your middle finger on the 2nd fret of the E string. This might feel a little awkward but there's a trick to doing it correctly. You still want your left-hand placement to stay the same (refer to the Getting Started section for a refresher on the proper placement) but you'll need to rotate your hand so that the angle allows you to still use your fingertips. To do this, simply move your left elbow away from your body while keeping the points of contact with the neck the same. This will move your hand in a way that accommodates playing across the strings like this. Do not, however, put your thumb behind the neck!

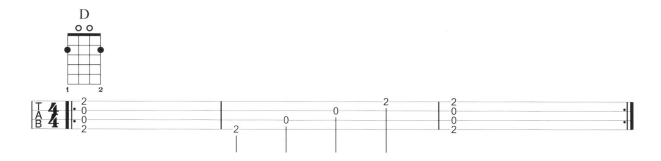

MINOR CHORDS: D MINOR (0:45–0:30) 🔊

Like all of the other minor chords, this one is only one note different from its major counterpart but we'll have to switch which fingers we're using to make it possible. Start by placing your index finger on the 1st fret of the E string. Then place your middle finger on the 2nd fret of the G string. You'll need to bring your elbow more towards your body to get the hand-angle right.

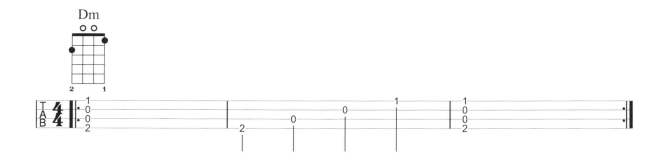

RHYTHM: WALTZ (0:30–0:15) 🔊

Most of what we'll talk about in this book is in 4/4 time, but there are lots of different time signatures. The most common one that you'll encounter, besides 4/4, is 3/4, which is sometimes called "waltz" time. Rather than four notes per measure (counted "1, 2, 3, 4"), waltz time has *three* beats (counted "1, 2, 3").

When playing rhythm in 3/4, we accent beats 2 and 3. If you mute the strings, you can practice this by playing a muted note on the G string, then two muted notes on the D string to hear where the accents should fall. Once you get this down, try adding an open G chord. Play a light note on the open G string on beat 1, then strum the chord on both beat 2 and beat 3.

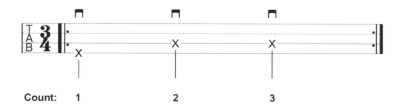

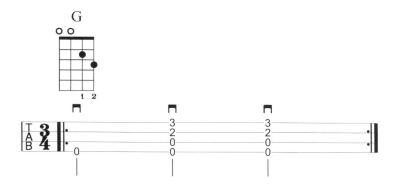

ORNAMENTS: PULL-OFF (0:15–0:00) 🔊

A *pull-off* is essentially the opposite of a hammer-on. We're still changing the pitch of a note with our left hand but we're going to do that by—you guessed it—pulling one of our fingers off of the string. Before we start, hold your instrument up and, with your left hand in its standard position, try to pluck one of the strings with your index finger. You might find it difficult to keep your hand in the proper position and get enough power by just flexing your finger, so, instead, try to rotate your forearm so that your finger is pulled through and away from the string.

Now let's try what's written. Put your index finger on the 2nd fret of the E string and pluck the note. Then, when the note is still ringing, rotate your forearm/wrist so that your finger plucks the sting. Try to keep your finger pressed down through the motion so that it sounds like one clean transition, without a pause in the middle.

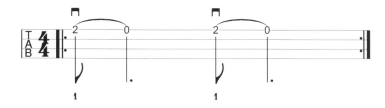

Now try adding the middle and ring fingers:

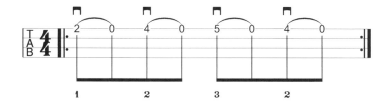

DAY 4

RIGHT HAND: PLAYING INSIDE THE STRINGS (1:30–1:15)

This exercise will help with playing eighth notes. Rather than having the pick go through the strings in a straight line, imagine the motion of painting something with a brush: you're looking for that subtle arch, with the string being right at the zenith. This motion will allow you to switch between strings without bumping into other strings or feeling like you have to lift your hand up to avoid them.

To perform this exercise, start with a downstroke on the open D string. Then we're going to perform an upstroke on the G string. Practice this slowly with a metronome. If you hit the other strings while playing, then slow the metronome down—and don't speed it back up until you've played this figure three times with no mistakes. Once you're able to play the first exercise cleanly, repeat the process on the A and D strings and then on the E and A strings.

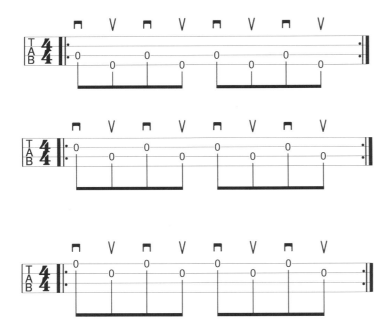

LEFT HAND: MUTING CHORDS WITH THE PINKY
(1:15–1:00)

Let's talk about muted notes. Most of the time, we're using the fingers on our left hand to push down a string to change its pitch. However, we can also place our fingers on a string without pushing down. If we play a note while our finger is on a string but not pushing down, it will make a percussive noise not associated with any note.

This is a useful technique when it comes to playing chords. Sometimes, we only want two or three notes to ring but we have four (courses of) strings.

Let's practice this next exercise by placing our left hand pinky around the 5th fret of the E string. It doesn't have to be exactly on the fret; just in that general area (because we're not trying to play an actual note). Rest your finger on the string but don't use enough pressure to push the string down. Now pick the E string with your right hand.

MAJOR CHORDS: CLOSED C MAJOR (1:00–0:45) 🔊

So far, all of the chords we've learned are in what we call "open position" because they use open strings. Open chords have a really powerful sound but are limited by the fact that they can't be moved because the open strings are always the same notes.

Conversely, a *closed-position chord* is one that doesn't use any open strings. The benefit of these chords is that the same fingerings can be used to voice many different chords. But, in order to do that, we usually have to use all four fingers, which is more challenging. However, we just learned a trick to help make the process easier—muting with our pinky.

We're going to learn a closed-position C chord, so let's start with the same fingering from our open-position C chord: index finger on the 2nd fret of the D string, middle finger on the 3rd fret of the A string. Now we're going to add our ring finger to the 5th fret of the G string. Technically, we could play these three notes with the open E string and it would still be a C major chord, but we don't want any open strings. Rather than trying to fret another note with our pinky, we're going to use our muting trick by placing our pinky on the E string, around the 5th fret, without pressing down. Now, when you strum this chord, you'll hear the three fretted notes but not the muted one.

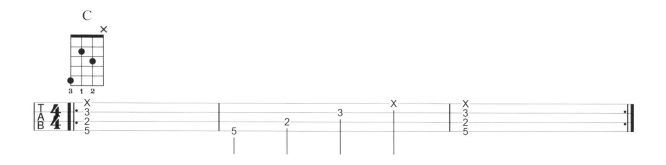

MINOR CHORDS: MUTED C MINOR (0:45–0:30) 🔊

Let's look at how to use the pinky muting technique to make our open C minor chord a little easier to play. Fret the notes of the open C minor chord and then mute the E string with the pinky. This will allow us to play all four strings without having to worry about the open E sounding bad.

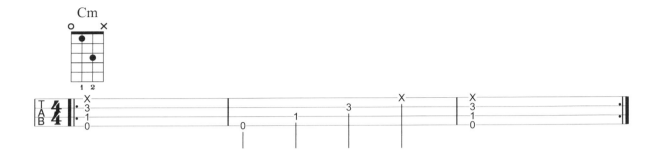

RHYTHM: INTRO TO CHOP (0:30–0:15) 🔊

The short rhythm sound often associated with bluegrass mandolin is called a "chop." The chop sound is created via slight movements in the left and right hands. Let's focus on the left hand today.

The left hand is what controls the length of the chop, or how long the notes are heard. For the short sound, all we're going to do is stop pressing down with the fingers on our left hand. Place your fingers into the closed C major chord shape. If you press down and strum the chord, the notes will keep ringing and trail off. If you strum the chord and then stop pressing down, the note will be cut short.

Practice this exercise while slowly counting "1, 2, 3, 4." Strum the chord on beats 1 and 3, and release the pressure on beats 2 and 4. Remember, you don't need to take your fingers off of the strings when you stop pressing.

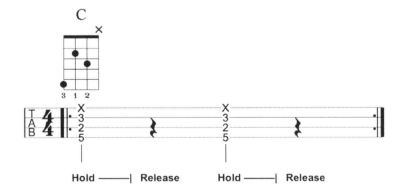

ORNAMENTS: INTRO TO TREMOLO (0:15–0:00) 🔊

Tremolo is a musical effect whereby a note is repeated very quickly. Rather than thinking of it as a bunch of individual notes, I find it is helpful to think of it like a violin bow. If the bow is on the string, the note will ring as long as the bow is pulled. But notes on the mandolin only ring for a limited amount of time. If we have to play a whole note, the note will likely trail off before we've finished all four counts. This is where tremolo comes in. Instead of just letting the note ring, we can play the note over and over again to fill in that space. There is no set number of notes we are trying to play in that space and, in fact, trying to count them will actually make it harder. Instead, just count "1, 2, 3, 4" while quickly alternating upstrokes and downstrokes on the open A string, like this:

Now try adding tremolo to every other beat:

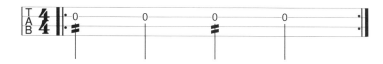

Finally, add tremolo to all four strings:

DAY 5

RIGHT HAND: PLAYING OUTSIDE THE STRINGS (1:30–1:15)

The exercises below are the same as the ones from yesterday, just reversed! Start with a downstroke on the open G string, then play an upstroke on the open D string. If you're using the curved paintbrush motion, you should be able to play through *both* G strings and *both* D strings without accidentally hitting any others. After a few passes through the first exercise, move on to the second one and, finally, the third one, repeating the picking motion (down-up, down-up, etc.) throughout.

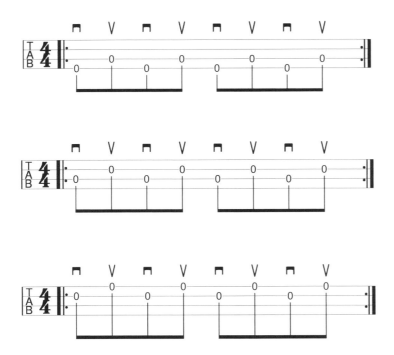

LEFT HAND: INDEX/RING FINGER CRAWL (1:15–1:00)

Let's try an exercise that will help with the strength of our ring finger and the agility needed for switching between different sets of fingers. Start with your index finger on the 1st fret of the G string (this is a particularly difficult note to fret, so, if you're struggling, don't worry—it's normal). Then play the 5th fret of the G string with your ring finger. Now play the 1st fret of the D sting with your index finger, and the 5th fret of the D sting with your ring finger. Continue to the A and E strings and then go back down. Practice slowly at first to get a good tone, but then add a metronome and try to keep time. For added challenge, try not to pick up your index finger when you put your ring finger down.

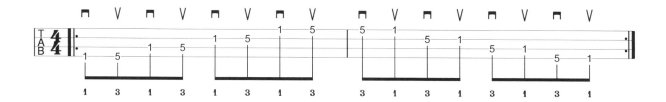

MAJOR CHORDS: CLOSED G MAJOR (1:00–0:45) 🔊

Let's learn a closed G major chord. We're going to keep using our pinky to mute one of the strings but our fingering will be a little different than the one used for our open G chord.

Start with your pinky muting the E string. Then place your middle finger on the 4th fret of the G string, your ring finger on the 5th fret of the D string, and your index finger on the 2nd fret of the A string.

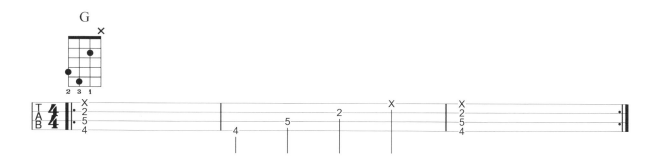

MINOR CHORDS: OPEN E MINOR (0:45–0:30) 🔊

Here's a new technique for playing chords. On the guitar, there is a chord technique called a "barre," which involves placing a single finger across two or more strings. We're going to do something similar but, because we have fewer strings, we usually only need to cover two strings with one finger. So, rather than laying our finger flat across the strings, we can use just our fingertip.

Take your index finger and place it in between the D and A strings at the 2nd fret. We are technically pressing down on four strings (two Ds and two As). If you have skinny fingers like mine, your fingertip won't fully cover all four strings, but that's OK. If you played each of the strings, the first D would be muted by your finger flesh, the second D would ring with the new pitch, the first A would ring with the new pitch and the second A would be muted by your finger flesh. Similar to our closed-position chords, these muted notes will not stick out when we play the notes together; in other words, we'll only hear the fretted ones.

Play this "barre" with the open G string and open E string and you have an open-position E minor chord.

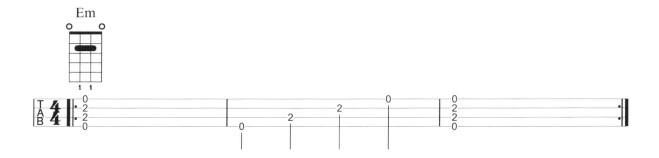

RHYTHM: CHOP (0:30–0:15) 🔊

Let's hone in on that chop rhythm. I mentioned that there are some things to pay attention to in the right hand. When strumming with the right hand, keep your wrist fairly loose and move your arm with the elbow. Then imagine using a whip as you move the pick through the strings. This will create the intensity needed.

As for the left hand, we're going to do the same thing as yesterday, only quicker. When you play the chord, let it ring for just a moment but then quickly release the pressure. There is no "correct" amount of time to let the note ring; experiment with it and see what different sounds and feelings you can create.

When chopping like this, we are working with the bass player to create a rhythm. If we're playing in 4/4 time, we'll count "1, 2, 3, 4." The bass is going to play a note on beats 1 and 3 (we can mimic the bass, as shown below), and we're going to chop on beats 2 and 4. In other words, we would count: 1, *chop*, 3, *chop*. (The dots above the chords are *staccato marks,* which indicated that the chords are to be played with a shortened attack, rather than allowing them to ring out for their full duration.)

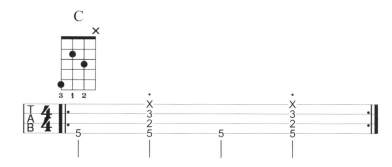

ORNAMENTS: TREMOLO TRIPLETS (0:15–0:00) 🔊

If the idea of playing an undetermined number of notes during a tremolo felt uncomfortable, you're in luck! In bluegrass, there is way to count tremolo (i.e., having a set number of notes) while still capturing the necessary feeling: triplets.

Triplets are three-note patterns that allow us to play three notes in a space usually reserved for two. To understand that idea, count out loud: "1-&, 2-&, 3-&, 4-&." Then, with that same feeling (and tempo), pronounce "triplet" with three syllables: "tri-pl-let, tri-pl-let, tri-pl-let, tri-pl-let" (or "1-&-a, 2-&-a, 3-&-a, 4-&-a").

The problem with triplets is that, because three notes are played on each beat, our pick direction gets thrown off momentarily because we've ended on a downstroke after one beat—right before a numbered count (beat 2). When playing tremolo, this problem sorts itself out because we are always going to be playing more than one triplet.

For example, if we have a whole note that we need to tremolo over, we could play four triplets and our pick direction would be "down-up-down, up-down-up, down-up-down, up-down-up." This has us ending with an upstroke so we're ready to play a downstroke on the next strong (numbered) beat (i.e., beat 1 of the next measure).

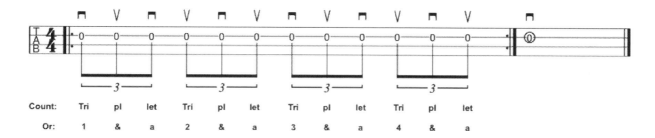

The same outcome occurs if we play two triplets. Notice in the example below that we arrive at a downstroke on beat 3—a strong (numbered) beat.

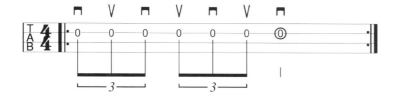

DAY 6

RIGHT HAND: COUNTRY RHYTHM (1:30–1:15) 🔊

Our next example is a simplified shuffle pattern that's really common in various forms of country music. In this exercise, we'll just be playing the open A string. Start by counting "1-&, 2-&, 3-&, 4-&." Then play on just the counts "1, 2-&, 3, 4-&," using a down, down-up, down, down-up picking pattern. Practice this exercise several times and then try adding emphasis to beats 1 and 3.

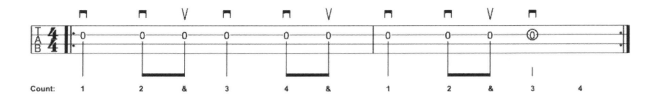

LEFT HAND: G MAJOR SCALE (1:15–1:00) 🔊

Remember the rules for fingers while playing this G major scale (G–A–B–C–D–E–F♯).

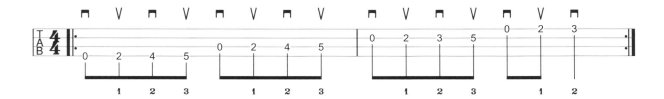

If you want an extra challenge, try using your pinky on the 7th fret of each string instead of playing the open strings, as both notes are the same pitch.

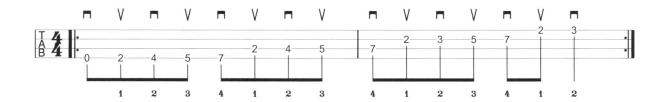

MAJOR CHORDS: CLOSED D MAJOR (1:00–0:45) 🔊

We learned the closed-position C major chord so that we could move the shape around without worrying about the open strings. To make this D major chord, you'll be using your pinky to mute the E string, but this time, try to place it around the 7th fret. Then use your ring finger to play the 7th fret of the G string, your index finger to play the 4th fret of the D string, and your middle finger to play the 5th fret of the A string. You'll notice that this is the same position your hand was in for the C major chord. In fact, if you keep your hand in that position and move each finger down (away from the bridge) two frets, you'll have a C chord.

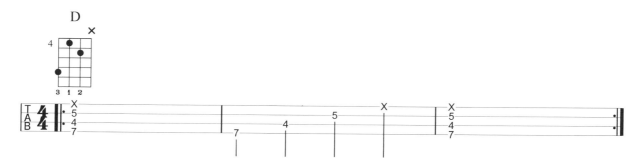

Not so hard, right? Let's learn a quick variation on that same chord. For this, we'll still be muting the E string with our pinky but now we can have it rest near the 5th fret. Then we'll place our index finger on the 2nd fret of the G string, our middle finger on the 4th fret of the D string, and our ring finger on the 5th fret of the A string. Notice that the two middle strings are the same notes as before.

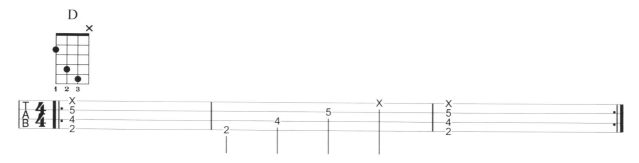

MINOR CHORDS: CLOSED D MINOR (0:45–0:30) 🔊

Similarly, the Dm chord is going to be the same as the C minor chord but two frets higher. The easiest way to find this chord is by making our D major chord (the first version from the previous section) and moving our index finger down one fret (away from the bridge) to fret 3 of the D string.

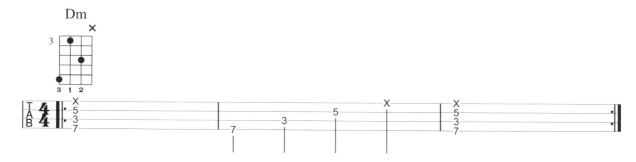

We can also use the variation that we learned to make a D minor chord. Start with the D major chord, then move your middle finger down one fret to fret 3 of the D string.

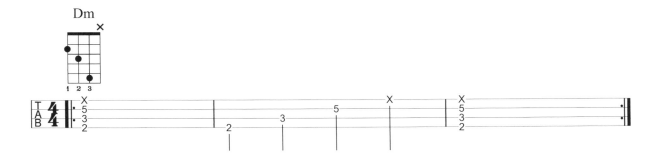

RHYTHM: SWITCHING CHORDS: G–D (0:30–0:15) 🔊

We've worked on different rhythms but now let's try switching between two different chords. We're going to use our variation of the D major chord and our simplified G major chord. First, make the chords one at a time and get the feeling in your hands. Notice how similar they are. The pinky is muting the E string in both chords, so you don't need to lift it up when you switch, and the fingers stay on the same frets but switch strings between the two chords.

We're going to use our boom-chuck rhythm, so start with two boom chucks of the G chord, then switch to the D chord and do two more boom chucks. Then repeat. At first, you only need to focus on comfortably switching between the two chords. But, eventually, you should turn on a metronome, set it to a slow tempo, and make sure that you don't slow down when you switch chords.

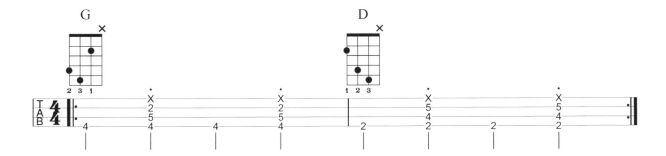

44

ORNAMENTS: DOWNWARD SLIDE (0:15–0:00) 🔊

The downward slide is, as you could guess, the same as the upward slide, just reversed. In other words, sliding *away* from the bridge. We'll practice by putting our ring finger on the 5th fret of the A string. Pluck the string and then, without lifting your finger, slide it to the 4th fret.

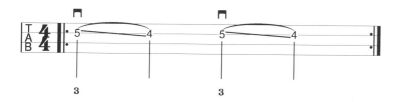

DAY 7

WEEK 1 REVIEW: PUTTING IT ALL TOGETHER (1:30–0:00)

Now it's time to have a little fun! This arrangement of the folk song "Angeline the Baker" incorporates much of the material that you've learned throughout the week. The top tab staff features the song's melody, while the bottom staff includes the chord changes, played in the boom-chuck rhythm. You can spend today's lesson on either part, or split your time between the two, but the goal is to eventually learn and memorize the tune completely, so you'll need to come back to it from time to time in order to do so.

ANGELINE THE BAKER

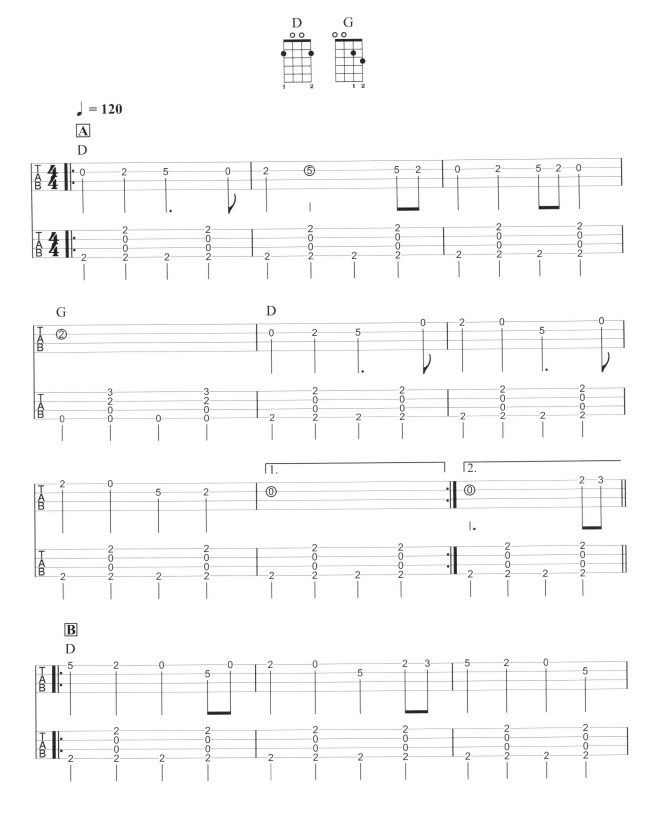

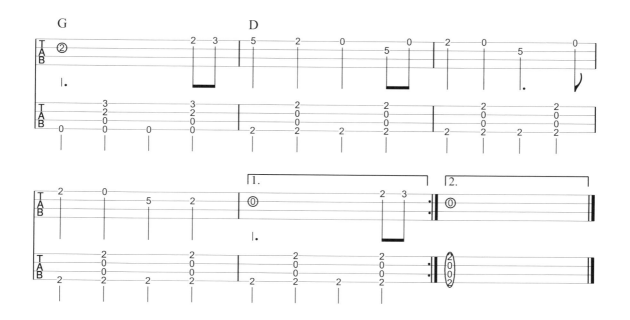

RIGHT HAND: TREMOLO PICKING TWO OPEN STRINGS  (1:30–1:15)

Today, we're going to practice our tremolo but using two open strings instead of one. All of the motions will be the same but your pick will move in a slightly larger arch to get both A and both E strings on each upstroke and downstroke.

LEFT HAND: A MAJOR SCALE (1:15–1:00)

Let's look at the A major scale (A–B–C♯–D–E–F♯–G♯). The first bit is index, middle, and ring fingers on the 2nd, 4th, and 6th frets of the G string, respectively, followed by the open D string. Then we do the same thing on the next string: index, middle, and ring on the 2nd, 4th, and 6th frets, followed by the open A string. That is one whole octave of the A major scale. For the second octave, we'll play the 2nd, 4th, and 5th frets of the A string, followed by the open E string, and then we'll end with the 2nd, 4th, and 5th frets of the E string. Notice the pattern here?

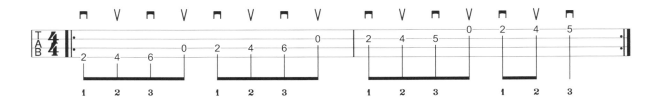

We can make the pattern even more obvious by adding our pinky. Start the same as before, playing the 2nd, 4th, and 6th frets on the G string with the index, middle, and ring fingers, respectively, and the 7th fret with the pinky. Then play exactly the same thing on the D string. For the A string, play the 2nd, 4th, and *5th* frets with the index, middle, and ring fingers, respectively, and the 7th fret with the pinky. Finally, finish up with the 2nd, 4th, and 5th frets on the E string.

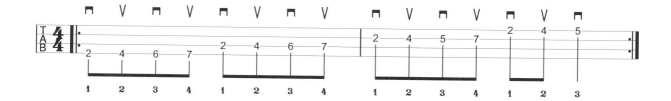

Notice that, when we added the 7th fret, we didn't use any of the open strings. This makes this scale position "closed," meaning we can move it around. In fact, what defines this pattern as a major scale is the specific pattern of whole steps (two frets) and half steps (one fret). More specifically, any major scale can be played by starting with the root note and then moving up by a whole step, whole step, half step, whole step, whole step, whole step, half step (W–W–H–W–W–W–H).

MAJOR CHORDS: OPEN A5 BARRE CHORD (1:00–0:45) 🔊

Do you remember the E minor chord, which required one finger to play two strings? Well, we're going to do that again, just with different strings. Place your index finger between the G and D strings at the second fret. When played along with the open A and E strings, you have an A chord! And what's interesting about this chord is that it's neither major nor minor, so it works in both situations! How is that possible? Well, you know how our minor chords have been the same as the major chord, just with one note moved down? That note is called the *mediant*, or "3rd." The 3rd in A major is C♯. In A minor, the 3rd is C (natural). The chord we just learned, A5, only contains the notes A and E, the root and 5th, respectively—there is no 3rd, so there is no way to distinguish it as major or minor!

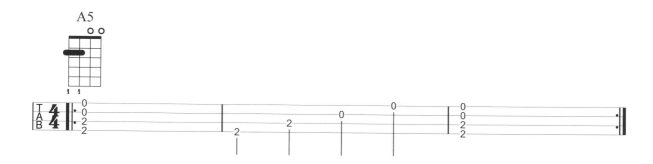

MINOR CHORDS: ADDING THE MIDDLE AND RING 🔊 FINGERS TO THE A5 CHORD (0:45–0:30)

But what if we wanted to make the A5 chord major or minor? Well, that's easy. The 3rd fret of the A string is a C, and the 4th fret is a C♯. So, if we want to make A5 an A minor, we simply add our middle finger to the 3rd fret of the A string. If we want to make it an A major, we can add our ring finger to the 4th fret of the A string.

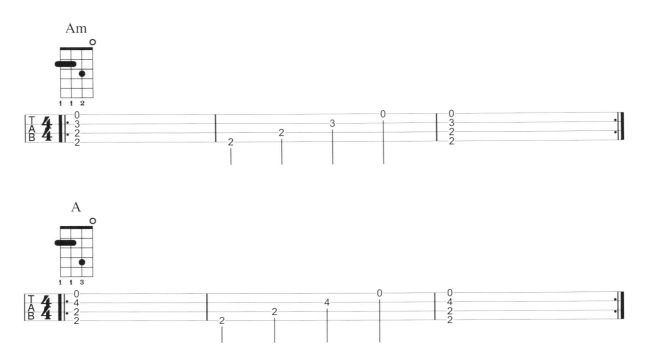

RHYTHM: ROCK CHOP (0:30–0:15) 🔊

The C major "chop" chord that we learned last week required us to use all four fingers so that we could mute the notes but there's a way to achieve this sound with open chords, as well. We're going to practice the basic movement for now. Start by making your one-finger A5 barre chord. We're going to play this chord and then mute all four strings by laying our ring and pinky fingers flat across the fretboard. We're not pressing down with those fingers, just covering the strings so they stop vibrating. Try playing a quarter-note downstroke through the chord and then muting on the next beat: 1 (ring), 2 (mute), 3 (ring), 4 (mute).

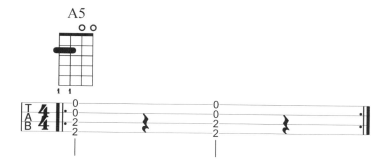

ORNAMENTS: DOUBLE-DOWNSTROKE TRIPLETS 🔊
(0:15–0:00)

Today is all about memory. Do you remember when we talked about triplets, and how one of the problems was that, because it's three notes, triplets can throw your pick direction out of sync? Well, there is a way around that by doing a "double-down triplet." This means you will play two downstrokes in a row to even out that pick direction. This is really hard to do on one string, so the best way to approach this is when you can go to another string.

Let's start with just open strings. Play a triplet on the A string. Remember, these three notes are going to take the time it normally takes to play two eighth notes, so we count it "1-&-a." The pick direction for this is down-up-down but the next beat is a number (beat 2) so we need to play a downstroke. So, play a downstroke on the open E string, as well. All together it would be counted "1-&-a, 2, 3-&-a, 4" and the pick would go: down-up-down, down, down-up-down, down.

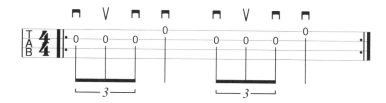

Now let's try it with some left-hand involvement. We're just going to play a "run" with the triplet but the count and pick direction will stay the same.

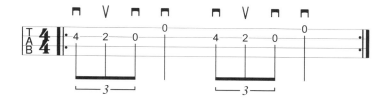

DAY 9

RIGHT HAND: EXERCISE FOR BUILDING CONTROL (1:30–1:15)

This exercise will help build control in our right hand, which we can use to accent notes for effect. We're going to play two eighth-note open-D-string pickup notes to start (*pickup notes* are notes that come in before the downbeat of the first measure). Then we're going to start our pattern of playing the open A string and two open D strings. We're going to do this four times before ending on an open A string and starting over with our pickup notes.

Since this is a three-note pattern, the open A note will alternate between landing on a numbered beat (on beat) and an "and" beat (off beat). At first, I want you to try playing this exercise so that the notes all sound consistent, with no accent placed on any note. Once you're able to do that, try placing an accent on all the open As. This will be easy when the open A is on beat, but when it switches to an off-beat, you'll have to accent the note with an upstroke.

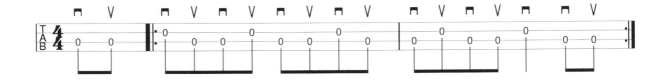

LEFT HAND: INTRO TO DOUBLE STOPS (1:15–1:00)

Double stops are a powerful tool that we can use to elevate our melodies. *Double stops* are two notes played at the same time. Since that definition is very open-ended, we'll say that, for our purposes, double stops are a melody note and a note that harmonizes with it, often from the key of the chord that the melody is being played over. In other words, if someone is playing an A chord, we're going to play our melody note, plus a note from the A chord to make a double stop that sounds nice.

Let's start by playing a one-octave A major scale. Then we're going to play an A major arpeggio (an *arpeggio* is simply the notes of a chord played individually). The notes in an A major chord are A, C♯, and E, which are the 1st, 3rd, and 5th notes of the A major scale: **A**–B–**C♯**–D–**E**–F♯–G♯. (Major chords are built from the 1st, 3rd, and 5th notes of their relative major scales, and minor chords are built from the 1st, 3rd, and 5th notes of their relative minor scales.)

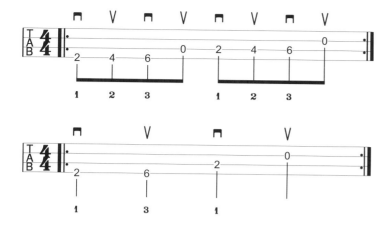

Next, let's add notes to our regular A major scale until we get to the high C♯ at the 9th fret of the E string.

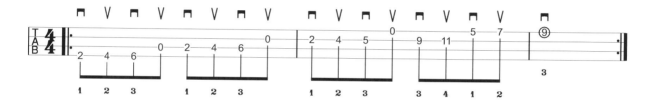

Remember, the 1st, 3rd, and 5th notes of the A major scale are A, C♯, and E. Now let's play our longer scale but with only those three notes; in other words, a longer A major arpeggio. Any combination of those three notes will work as a double stop in the key of A major.

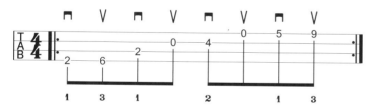

(You'll notice that, when we start playing notes above the 7th fret, we have to shift our hand up and use our index finger to play the notes our ring finger usually plays. This is called 3rd position. The best time to shift is when there is an open string being played. Since you don't need to use your left hand to play the note, it's free to move up the neck and get set for 3rd position).

Let's use two notes from the A major arpeggio to learn a simple double stop. Your index finger will play the E note at the 2nd fret of the D string, and your middle finger will play the C♯ note at the 4th fret of the A string. Since these two strings are right next to each other, we can play through both D strings and both A strings in one downstroke.

MAJOR CHORDS: CLOSED A MAJOR BARRE CHORD 🔊 (1:00–0:45)

We've already seen the versatility of the A5 barre chord, but this next trick takes it over the top. By turning it into a closed-position chord, we can play nearly every major and minor chord with very little effort.

To start, make the barre with your index finger on the 2nd fret of both the G and D strings. Then we're going to make this a major chord by adding our ring finger to the 4th fret of the A string. Finally, we'll use our pinky to play the 5th fret of the E string. This is a closed-position A major chord but notice how our index finger is sort of pointing to the A note at the 2nd fret of the G string. We can keep this shape and move the chord around so whatever note your index finger is pointing at, that's what major chord you're playing!

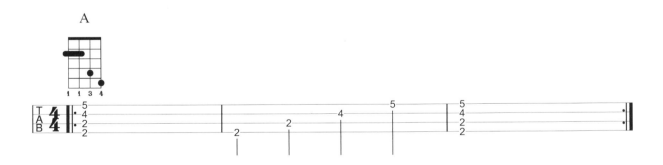

MINOR CHORDS: CLOSED A MINOR BARRE CHORD 🔊 (0:45–0:30)

Making a minor chord this way is just as easy. Start by making the closed A major barre chord that we just learned. Then lift up your ring finger and put your middle finger on the 3rd fret of the string. You should have your index finger on the 2nd fret of the G and D strings, your middle finger on the 3rd fret of the A string, and your pinky on the 5th fret of the E string. This is a closed A minor barre chord, which can be moved around in the same way as the A major barre chord to make any other minor chord.

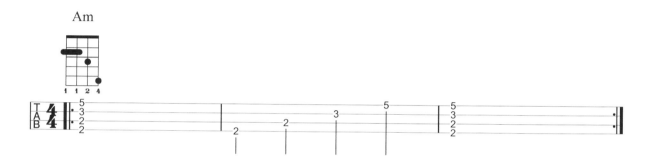

RHYTHM: ROCK CHOP – ADDING THE CHOP (0:30–0:15) 🔊

Now that we have the basic motion of muting an open chord with our ring and pinky fingers down, let's look at changing the timing to create more of a chop sound. We're going to be playing a rhythm similar to the boom chuck. Start by making your open A5 barre chord. We're going to count this "1, 2, 3, 4." On the count of 1, lightly play the G string with a downstroke (this is mostly just to help us keep time). Then, on the count of 2, play a downstroke through all of the strings while, at the same time, bringing your left-hand ring and pinky finger down to mute the chord. Play the G string lightly on count 3 and do another downstroke with the mute on count 4. It will take some practice to get the timing just right, but what you're trying to do is have your right hand arrive just ahead of your left so the notes ring out for just a moment before they're cut off.

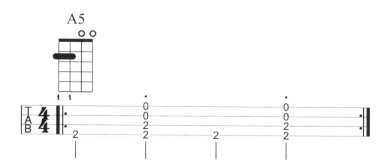

ORNAMENTS: TRIPLETS WITH HAMMER-ONS (0:15–0:00)

We've talked about triplets a bit already and how they can throw off our pick direction. Using this trick, we can add that third note without changing what our right hand is doing.

We're going to be practicing a pattern on the A string. Start by play the triplet pattern with alternating strokes as written. Notice how we have to use two downstrokes in a row to make it work and how that can throw off our timing. What we're going to do is add a hammer-on to get that middle note.

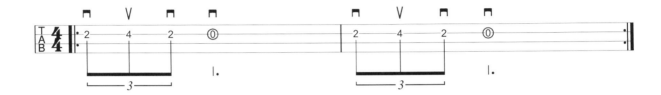

Start by playing the B note (index finger, 2nd fret, A string) with a downstroke. Then hammer onto C♯ (middle finger, 4th fret, A string). Next, play that B note with an upstroke and end on the open A string with a downstroke. The timing of this might be tricky at first. To check if it's correct, try taking out the middle note; in other words, play two B notes, followed by the open A (counted "1-&, 2," and picked: down-up, down). Then keep that same timing but add the hammer-on between the two B notes.

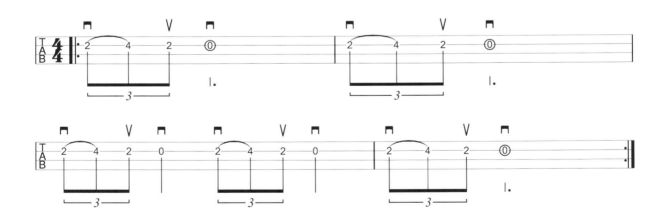

DAY 10

RIGHT HAND: DOUBLE STOPS WITH TREMOLO 🔊 (1:30–1:15)

Today, we're going to practice playing a double stop with tremolo. We're going to use the same double stop as yesterday (index finger, 2nd fret, D string, and middle finger, 4th fret, A string), and you can use either version of tremolo (free form or triplet tremolo). We just want to practice getting that steady tremolo sound out of the two notes, as well as accurately hitting just those two strings.

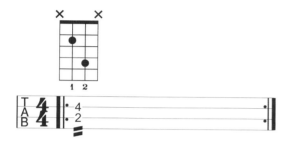

LEFT HAND: DOUBLE STOPS IN A MAJOR (1:15–1:00) 🔊

Let's go through and find a bunch of different double stops for the key of A major. First, let's refresh ourselves on the notes from the A major arpeggio.

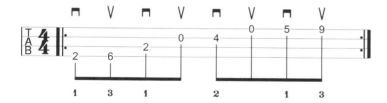

Then, to find the double stops, we're going to start with the first note (A, 2nd fret of the G string) and look for the next one of these notes that we could play at the same time. That note happens to be E (2nd fret of the D string). When we play those two notes together, you should notice that it's the same fingering as our A5 barre chord. If you go through these steps, you might end up with a pattern like the one below. Those double stops are derived entirely from the A major scale in 1st position.

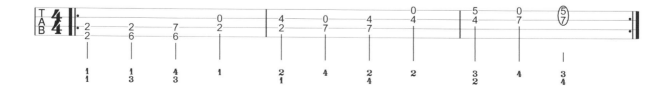

57

The next set involves a transition up to third position to get some other double stops. Even though we're playing different frets, all of the double stops are still combinations of the same three notes: A, C♯, and E. And, because we know that the 7th fret of each string is the same note as the open pitch of the next string, the notes above the 7th fret are the same notes as the ones above the next open string. Therefore, when we play the 11th fret of the D string and the 7th fret of the A string (C♯ and E, respectively), we're playing the same notes as when we play the 4th fret of the A string and the open E string (C♯ and E).

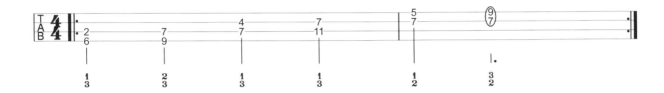

MAJOR CHORDS: E MAJOR BARRE CHORD (1:00–0:45)

Let's close the E barre chord the same way we did the A. Start by making your E barre—that is, by fretting both the D and the A strings at the 2nd fret with your index finger. Then we're going to put our middle finger on the 4th fret of the G string and our ring finger on the 4th fret of the E string. To get your fingers at the right angle to do this, without changing your left-hand position, keep your wrist straight while moving your elbow away from your body. This will rotate your hand into a more comfortable angle.

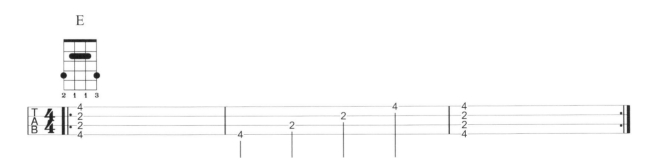

58

Below is a variation of the E major barre chord that we can also try. The fingering is slightly different, though. Our index finger will go to the 1st fret of the G string, and our middle finger will make the barre at the 2nd fret of the D and A strings. Then, we can use either our ring finger or our pinky to play the 4th fret of the E string. This chord is less common but I wanted to point out how useful the 1st fret of the G string is when playing in the key of E!

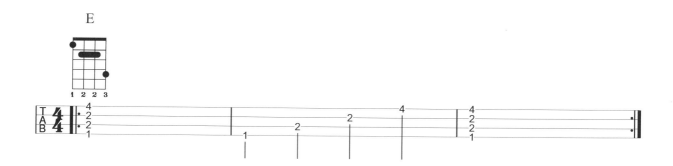

MINOR CHORDS: E MINOR BARRE CHORD (0:45–0:30) 🔊

The Em barre is similar to the major one but our fingers are going to switch. Start by making the barre on the D and A strings with your index finger. Then, this time, we're going to use our ring finger to play the 4th fret of the G string, which will put our middle finger in an advantageous position to play the 3rd fret of the E string. This fingering shouldn't require you to rotate your hand, so you can keep your elbow closer to your body, but make sure your wrist is still straight.

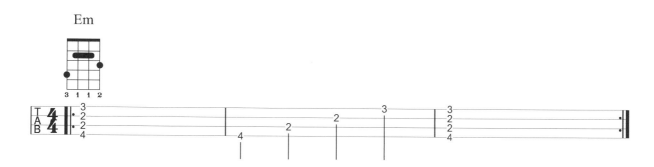

RHYTHM: A–E–D9 ROCK CHOP (0:30–0:15) 🔊

Muting chords with our ring and pinky finger works really well with the open A chord, but there are a few others we can use, as well. If we play the E barre chord that we just learned but leave the E string open, we can play it using this same method.

We can also play something close to a D chord this way. With your index finger on the 2nd fret of the G string, and all other strings open, we have what we might call a pseudo D9 chord. This chord can also be chopped in this way.

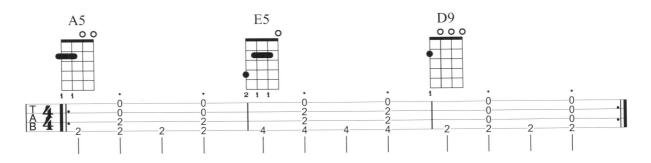

ORNAMENTS: SLIDING INTO DOUBLE STOPS (0:15–0:00) 🔊

Double stops can add a lot of depth to our melodies. By sliding into them, we can give those phrases a more lyrical feel. We're going to be working with our original double stop, which featured our index finger on the 2nd fret of the D string, and our middle finger on the 4th fret of the A string. We're going to play a measure of eighth notes (counted "1-&, 2-&, 3-&, 4-&," etc.), picking through both strings on both the downstrokes and the upstrokes. The catch will be that we will play notes one fret lower on the very first downstroke. So, put your index finger on the 1st fret of the D string, and your middle finger on the 3rd fret of the A string. Play those two notes with your first downstroke, then, without lifting your fingers from the strings, slide them up to the 2nd and 4th frets and play the upstroke.

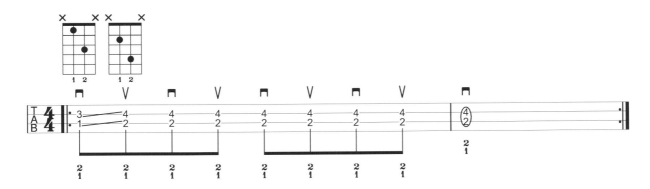

Sliding into both notes is a totally acceptable way to achieve the sound we're going for, but there is another, slightly more slick way: we're going to slide into just one of the notes. So, instead of starting on the 1st and 3rd frets, keep your index finger on the 2nd fret of the D string the whole time while starting with your middle finger on the 3rd fret of the A string. These notes will be the ones for the first downstroke and then you'll slide only your middle finger up the fretboard for the rest of the phrase. This creates a nice dissonance that is quickly resolved.

In practice, if you're going to use only one note to slide, you should slide the melody note while keeping constant the note that's harmonizing the melody.

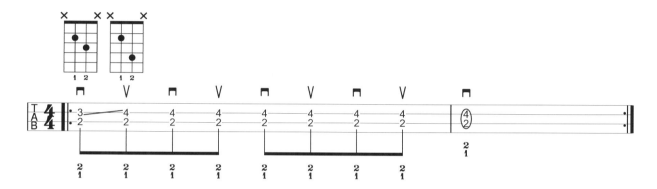

DAY 11

RIGHT HAND: OPEN-STRING TREMOLO DRONE (1:30–1:15)

Since we just practiced playing strings of double stops, this next bit should be a walk in the park. We're going to take a note and make it a double stop by harmonizing it with an open string. This is a common technique in the key of A but can be used any time the open strings work to create a harmony.

We're going to start by using our pinky to voice the 7th fret of the A string and playing the open E string at the same time. These notes are both Es but will (probably) not be *exactly* in tune with each other, which will create a cool-sounding effect.

Now try playing a measure of eighth notes with these notes:

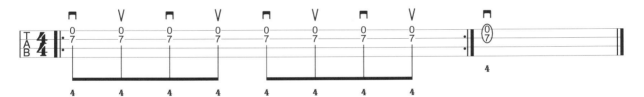

Next, let's do that same thing but add our sliding technique. So, our first notes will be the pinky on the 6th fret of the A string and the open E string, and then we'll slide our pinky up to the 7th fret on the first upstroke.

This sound is *very* important in bluegrass and country, as it imitates an effect commonly played on the fiddle.

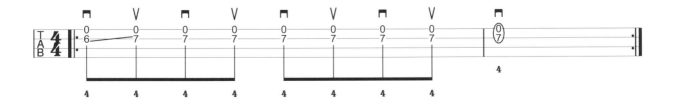

62

LEFT HAND: EASY I–M–R–P CRAWL (1:15–1:00) 🔊

We're going to start working towards the mother of all left-hand exercises. Although we'll be taking it slow for now, we're still going to work out all four fingers, as well as use alternating pick strokes: down-up, down-up, etc.

Start with your index finger on the first fret of the G string. Then place your middle finger on the 2nd fret of the G string without lifting your index finger from the string. It doesn't have to keep pressing down but practice keeping it in place while you put a new finger down. Next, place your ring finger on the 3rd fret of the G string and, once again, don't lift up either of the two previous fingers. Finally, place the pinky on the 4th fret of the G string.

Now we're going to move to the D string, but pay attention, because we're only going to move one finger at a time. At this point, all four of your fingers should be on the G string. Lift *only* your index finger and move it to the first fret of the D string. Then lift only your middle finger and move it to the second fret of the D string. Now move only your middle finger to the 3rd fret (this one will be hard). Finally, move only your pinky. Now all four fingers should be on the D string. Continue this pattern on the A and E strings.

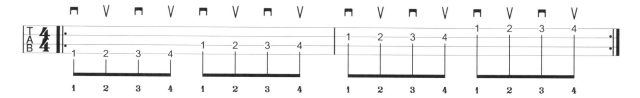

MAJOR CHORDS: G CHOP CHORD (1:00–0:45) 🔊

Here it is folks: the G chop chord! It's a peculiar way to play a G chord but the music has developed around this particular version. Let's start with our open G chord so we'll have our index finger on the 2nd fret of the A string and our middle finger on the 3rd fret of the E string. Now we're going to add our ring and pinky fingers. Place your ring finger on the 5th fret of the D string. Finally, place your pinky on the 7th fret of the G string. The pinky is the tricky part because we need to be using our fingertip; otherwise, it will mute the other strings. Don't worry if it doesn't come right away. For many folks, getting their hands to stretch this way takes years.

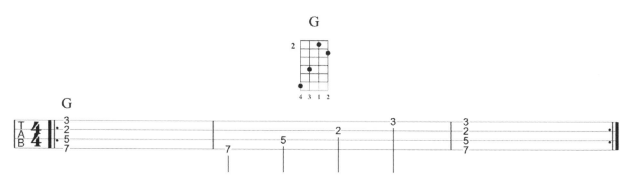

MINOR CHORDS: F♯ MINOR (0:45–0:30) 🔊

I loved learning this chord for some reason; there was just something so logical about it. F♯m is an important chord in the A major chord family, so it comes up fairly regularly in that key. The easiest way to play it is with our ring finger on the 6th fret of the G string, middle finger on the 4th fret of the D string, open A string, and index finger on the 2nd fret of the E string. If you want to practice the position we will use for the G chop chord in the future, try playing this with your pinky on the 6th fret, ring finger on the 4th fret, and middle finger on the 2nd fret.

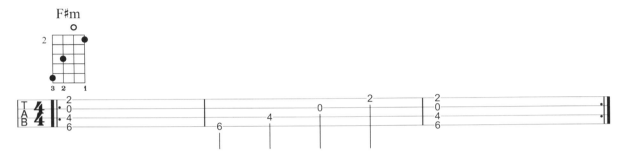

Obviously, this is an open-position chord, so, if we want to chop with it, we need to use a closed-position version, which can be created by barring our index finger across the D and A strings at the 4th fret, using our ring finger on the 6th fret of the G string, and our middle finger on the 5th fret of the E string. Notice how this is the same chord shape as our Em barre chord, just moved up two frets.

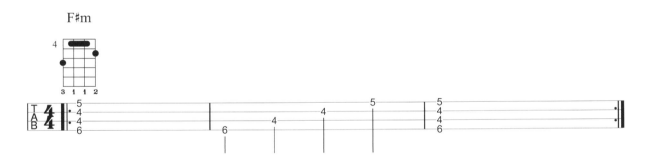

RHYTHM: "EARLY MONROE STRUM" IN A (0:30–0:15) 🔊

Let's say you're not interested in chopping but you want to play bluegrass. There are other options! The chop is really similar to someone hitting a snare drum but a lot of earlier bluegrass had a softer, more rhythmic approach to rhythm. We're going to learn a simplified version of that.

We are essentially going to be playing double-stop rhythms like we have before, only on the lower strings. Playing in the lower register will keep us from getting in the way of the singer or soloist. We can also use more of our arm to get some more power in the beats we want to emphasize.

We're in fourth position, so start with your index finger on the 7th fret of the D string, and your middle finger on the 9th fret of the G string. We'll call this "A." The rhythm we're going to play should be counted "1, 2-&, 3, 4-&," and picked down, down-up, down, down-up. While playing this pattern, try emphasizing beats 1 and 3.

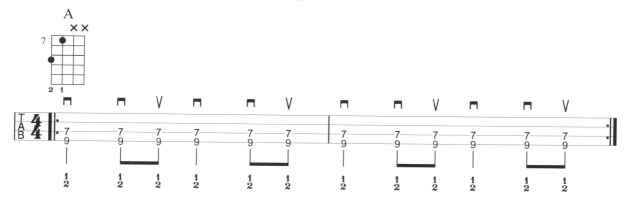

ORNAMENTS: HAMMER-ON/PULL-OFF TRIPLETS (0:15–0:00)

The previous triplet we learned made it so we only had to pick two of the three notes in the triplet. Now we're going to learn a way that requires picking just one of the notes! We'll start by using open strings because it's a little easier.

First, play your open E string. Then we're going to use our index finger to hammer onto the 2nd fret of the E string. Then, immediately after that, we are going to perform a pull-off to the open string. This all has to be done smoothly so that the string keeps vibrating for all three notes. That said, try to get the timing right (remember, the feel should sound like "trip-pl-let") and then add the ring finger to the 5th fret of the E string (this will make the timing "1-&-a, 2," etc.).

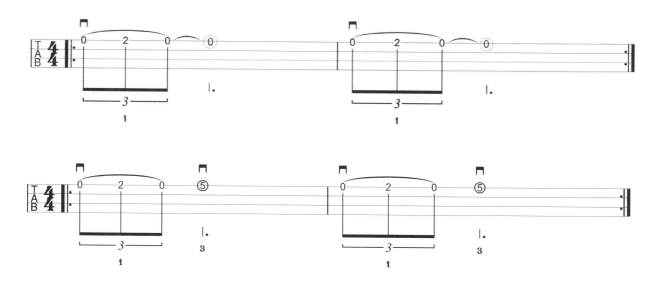

DAY 12

RIGHT HAND: CROSSPICKING (1:30–1:15) 🔊

In bluegrass music, banjos are traditionally performed with three fingers on the right hand playing a semi-constant stream of notes in patterns called "rolls." They play these eighth-note patterns all the time, even over vocal melodies that have longer sustained notes. Instead of playing a bunch of random notes, however, they are often playing the same notes over and over in a kind of drone. We can do the same thing on the mandolin to add interest while melody notes are sustained—without having to tremolo or play variations. We're going to learn one basic pattern, but there's a whole world of thought on how to play this style.

For our purposes, we're going to remain in the key of A. In the interest of keeping things simple, we'll use our open strings as drones (the open A and open E strings sound great in the key of A). Our melody note will be the E note played with the index finger on the 2nd fret of the D string. Play that as a downstroke, then the open A as an upstroke, followed by the open E as a downstroke and then the open A as an upstroke. Then you will be back at your first note and can repeat the pattern or move on to something else (but, for the sake of practice, let's just keep playing that pattern).

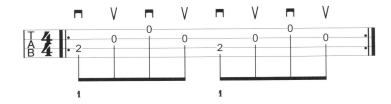

You can add other notes to this pattern without changing much. In the next example, the right hand does exactly the same thing—we just change what note we're playing when we get to the D string.

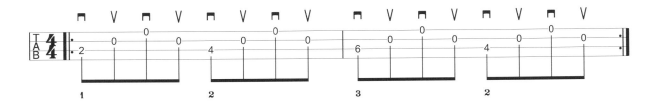

66

LEFT HAND: I–M–R–P CRAWL (1:15–1:00) 🔊

Today's version of the crawl is really similar to yesterday's—with one extra step. Today, we'll crawl up to the E string by only lifting up our fingers when needed (as before). Then, once all four of our fingers are down on the E string, we'll perform the whole exercise in reverse. The trick here will be lifting only one finger from the fingerboard at a time, as well as keeping the fingers within an inch of the string. We don't want our fingers to fly away from the string every time we pick them up, so practice keeping them as close to the string as possible at all times.

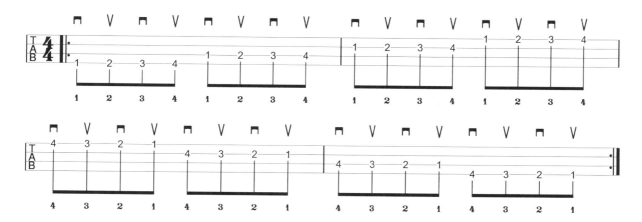

MAJOR CHORDS: INVERTED D CHOP CHORD (1:00–0:45) 🔊

Here's a new chord shape that is really convenient when switching to and from the G chop chord shape. Let's start by making a G chop chord. Our pinky is going to stay in the same place (the 7th fret of the G string). Our index finger will stay on the 2nd fret but move over to the E string, and then our middle and ring fingers will come to the middle strings—specifically, the 4th fret of the D string and the 5th fret of the A string, respectively.

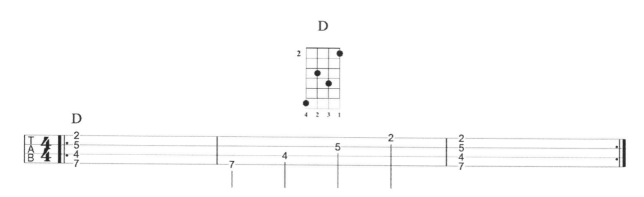

MINOR CHORDS: C MINOR BARRE CHORD (0:45–0:30)

Let's look at a way we can use the Am barre chord shape to play a different minor chord. Like I said, the chord will be whatever our index finger is pointing at, so let's point at a C note on the G string. Create a barre between the G and D strings at the 5th fret with your index finger. Then add your middle finger to the 6th fret of the A string and the pinky to the 8th fret of the E string. Notice that this is the same finger position as the Am chord, just moved up three frets!

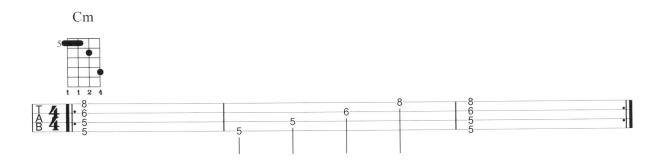

RHYTHM: MONROE STRUM: A–D (0:30–0:15)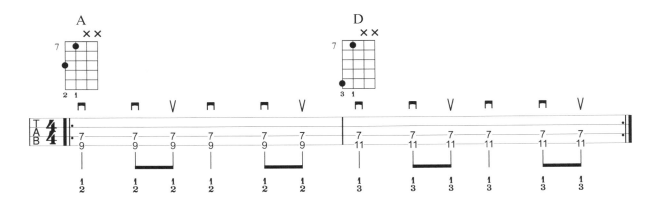

We're going to add another double stop to the strum pattern from yesterday and it will sound like we're switching chords. We'll start with the double stop we called "A." Then we'll follow the advice from our left-hand practice and keep both fingers down while adding the ring finger to the 11th fret of the G string. We'll call this second double stop "D." Play one measure of A and one measure of D and then repeat.

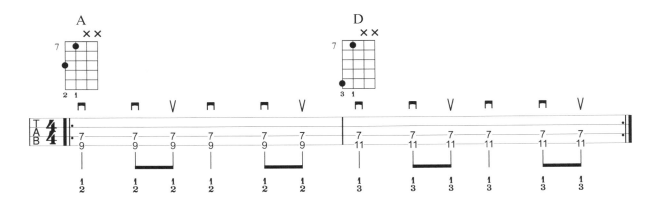

68

ORNAMENTS: CLOSED PULL-OFF (0:15–0:00) 🔊

So far, all of the pull-offs we've practiced have been a pull-off to an open string. Let's practice a closed pull-off, which involves pulling off to another fretted note. In the exercise below, we're going from C♯ (middle finger, 4th fret of the A string) to B (index finger, 2nd fret of the A string). Put both of the fingers down on their respective frets, play the 4th fret note (with a downstroke), and then pull off to the 2nd fret. Close it out by playing the open A string (with a downstroke), then repeat.

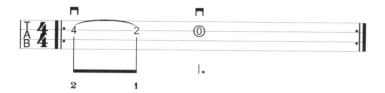

DAY 13

RIGHT HAND: OPEN-STRING DRONE AND MELODY 🔊 (1:30–1:15)

Once again, we're going to play through both the A and E string, but the melody will be performed on just the A string. Our right hand will be playing eighth notes on both strings while our left hand plays the melody. Practice with just the melody first and then add the open E string drone.

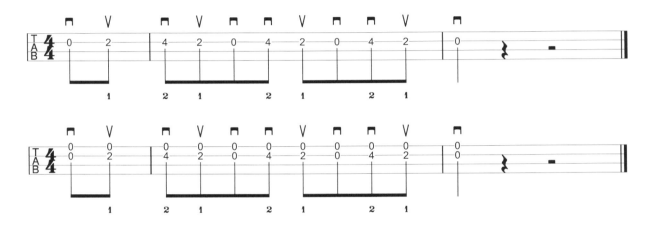

LEFT HAND: THE CRAWL (1:15–1:00) 🔊

Here's the full crawl. If you work on this exercise regularly, your left-hand technique will improve, including with your speed, tone, and control. We're going to go through each of the following steps:

1. Play the 1st, 2nd, 3rd, and 4th frets of the G string with your index, middle, ring, and pinky fingers, respectively. Make sure that you don't pick your fingers up as you go. You should end with all four fingers on the G string.

2. Now go backwards. Play the 4th fret, then lift up your pinky so you can play the ring finger, and so on. Don't let your fingers get too far away from the fretboard; try to keep them all within one inch of the string the entire time.

3. Now we're going work on our agility by adding a step. You should have your index finger down and the other three fingers floating above the string. Play the index finger again, then play the 4th fret with the pinky. Then the ring finger, followed by pinky. Then middle finger, pinky finger, ring finger, pinky finger. You should end up with all four fingers back on the string. Remember our rules about only moving the finger you need—not lifting fingers between notes—and keeping our fingers close to the string. (The full pattern is index, pinky, ring, pinky, middle, pinky, ring, pinky).

70

4. Now we're going to move to the next string and repeat the first three steps. Remember to only lift up the fingers you need, so start with only the index finger and move it over to the D string. Complete these steps on all four strings.

5. Once you finish the E string, lift up all of your fingers, except for your index finger. Slide the index finger up to the 2nd fret and play that note. Then, go through the first three steps—but using the 2nd, 3rd, 4th, and 5th frets on the E string.

6. When you finish, all four fingers should be down on the E string. Now carefully move to the A string while following our rules. You should end up with all four fingers on the G string at the 2nd, 3rd, 4th, and 5th frets. You can continue this exercise up the fretboard if you wish or end here.

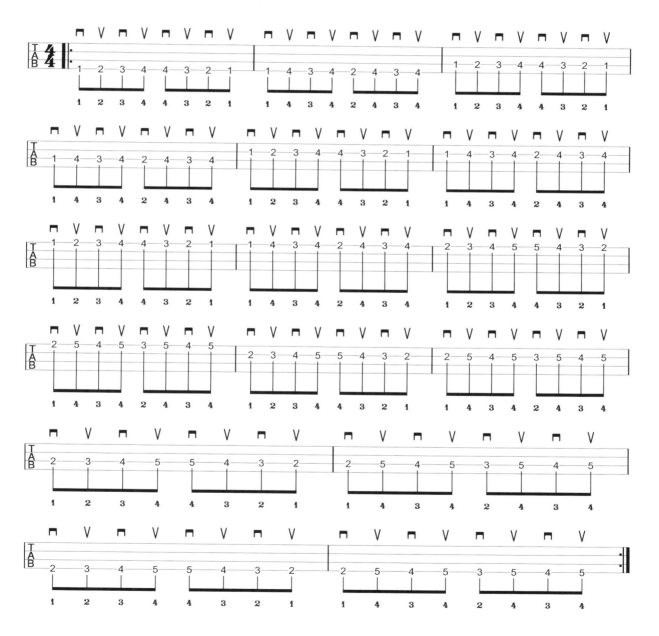

MAJOR CHORDS: A CHOP (1:00–0:45) 🔊

Let's try our big chop chord shape in a different place. We'll start with the index finger on the 4th fret of the A string, middle finger to the 5th fret of the E string, ring finger on the 7th fret of the D string, and pinky on the 9th fret of the G string. This is the same position as our G chop chord but a whole step (two frets) higher so it's an A chord. This should be a little easier to play because the frets are a little closer together.

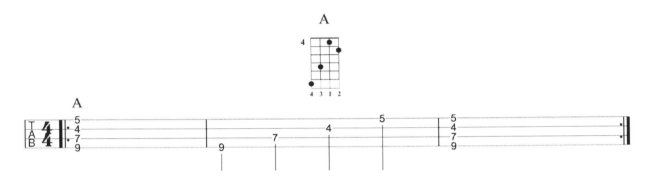

MINOR CHORDS: A DOMINANT SEVENTH (0:45–0:30) 🔊

At this point, we've learned the shapes that we would use to make a minor chord on the mandolin. Let's take this time before our last day to learn an easy way to play a dominant seventh chord. We're specifically going to look at an A dominant seventh chord, which is commonly called an "A7" chord. This will be the three notes of an A major chord, plus the ♭7 note. The 7th note of the A major scale is G♯, so we're going to add a G *natural* to our major triad.

Start by making your A barre chord by playing the 2nd fret of the G and D strings with your index finger. Then add your ring finger to the 4th fret of the A string to make it a major chord. Now, to add the ♭7 note, place your middle finger on the 3rd fret of the E string. As you can see, this is just another variation of the closed barre shape and can be moved around to make other 7th chords as needed.

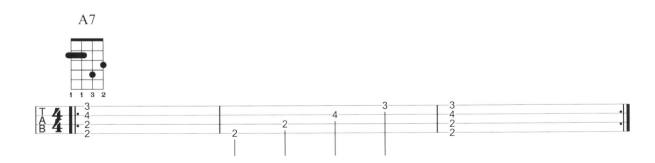

RHYTHM: MONROE STRUM: A–D–A–E (0:30–0:15) 🔊

So far, we've learned shapes that we're calling "A" and "D" with this strum pattern. If we were in the key of A, then A and D would be the I (1) and IV (4) chords. Most songs use the I (1), IV (4), and V (5) chords, so let's learn the V. In the key of A, the V (5) chord is E. It's really similar to the shape we're calling "A," just with the index finger moved down one fret. You could play this with your index and middle fingers and have it be a bit of a stretch, or you could play it with your index and ring fingers. The trick there is to make the transition to those new fingers sound smooth.

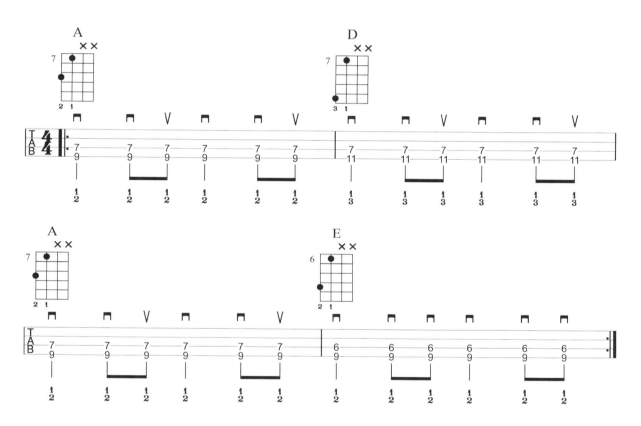

ORNAMENTS: CLOSED HAMMER-ON/PULL-OFF TRIPLETS (0:15–0:00)

Let's use the closed-position pull-off to create a closed-position hammer-on/pull-off triplet. We're going to be on the A string the whole time. We start with a downstroke and the index finger on the 2nd fret, then the middle finger hammers onto the 4th fret. Next, we'll pull the middle finger off and back to the index finger and end with the open A string. This should all be one fluid motion. You could think of it as your middle finger flicking that 4th fret.

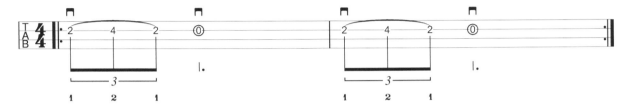

Depending on how you space out these notes, this kind of triplet can be a really common ornament known as a "trill" (or at least a simplified version of one). Traditionally, a trill involves notes that are right next to each other, which can give us some more of that quickly-resolved dissonance that we like. Try to achieve that sound by doing these same motions but using your middle finger to hammer onto and pull off of the 3rd fret.

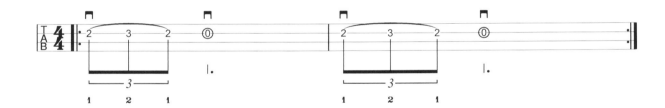

DAY 14

WEEK 2 REVIEW: PUTTING IT ALL TOGETHER (1:30–0:00)

Congratulations! You made to Day 14, the last day of the two-week program! Today, we're going to spend the entire 90 minutes playing through and learning the New Year's staple "Auld Lang Syne." Like "Angeline the Baker," this arrangement features both the melody and rhythm parts—in this case, a chop rhythm—and incorporates much of the material you practiced throughout the past two weeks, particularly Week 2. One exception, however, is the E chord. Although technically new, this chord is voiced the same way as the inverted D chord from Day 12, just two frets higher on the neck. Split your practice session between the two parts to keep the session fresh. You likely won't learn the entire song in one sitting, so can come back to it occasionally until you do. Good luck!

74

AULD LANG SYNE

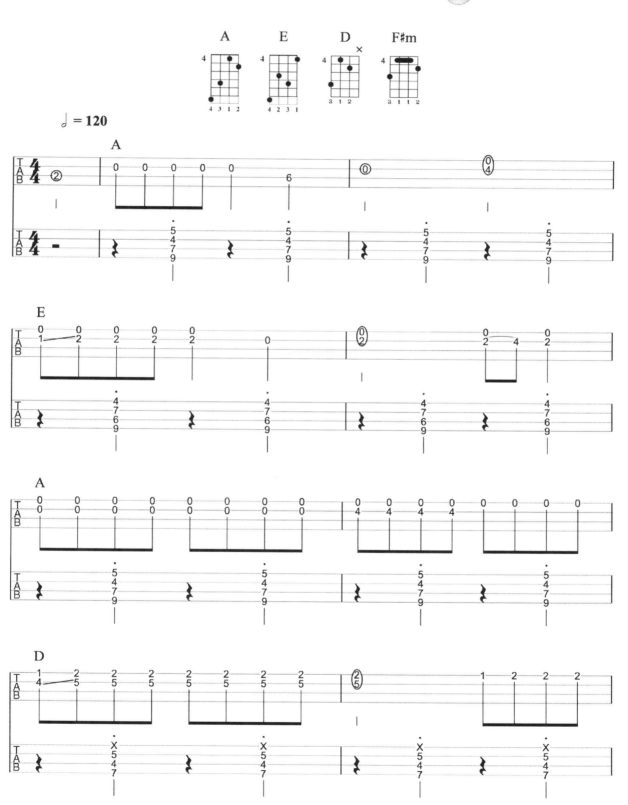

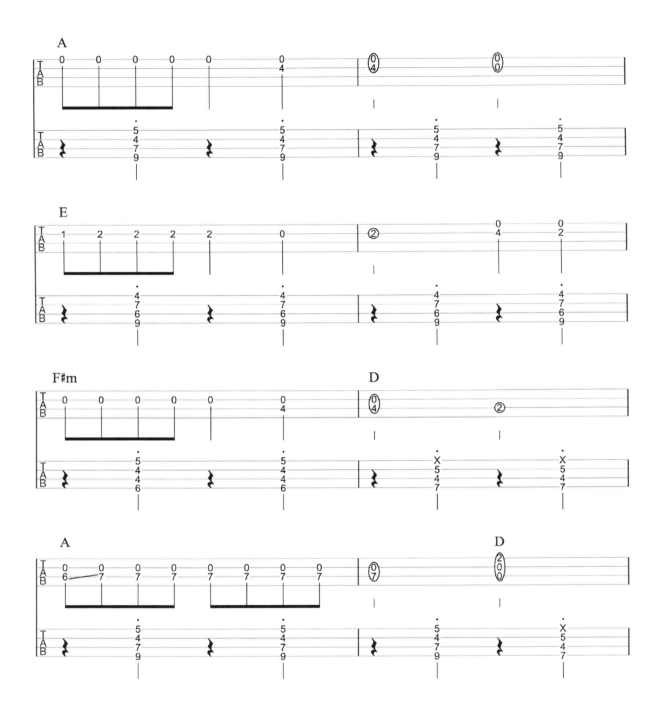

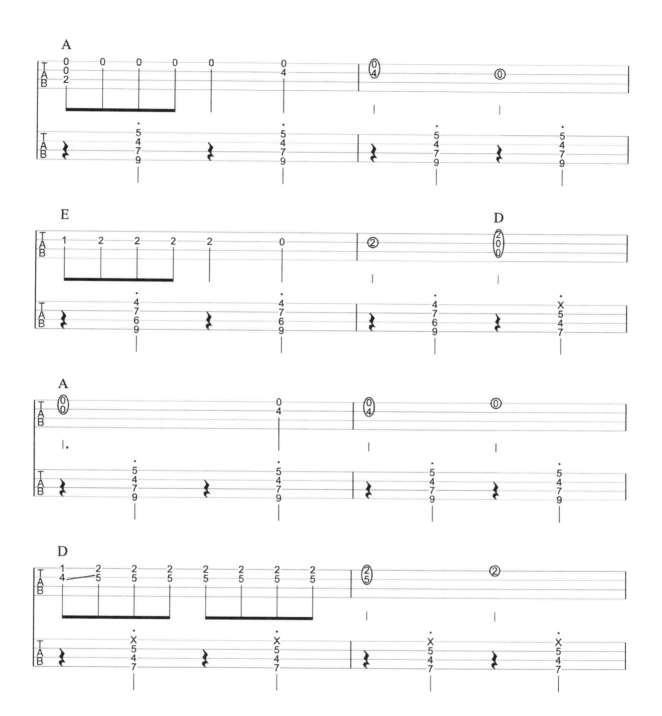

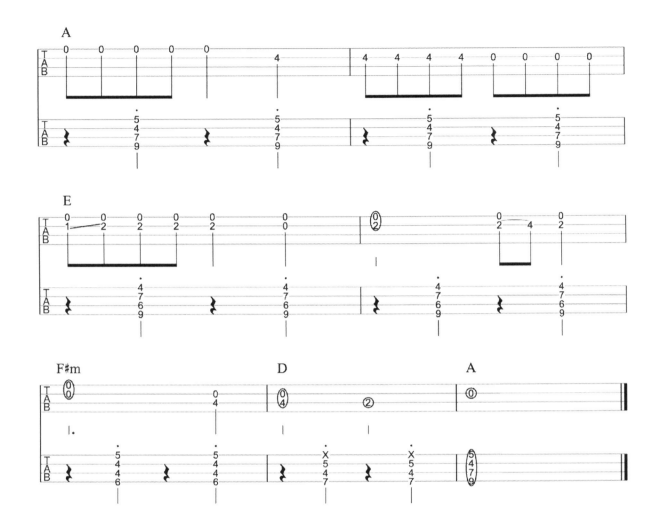

MOVING FORWARD

As you continue to learn the mandolin, I would highly recommend finding a teacher or mentor. Making progress involves setting goals and being able to identify when you are moving towards or away from those goals. A good teacher can help with both of those things as you develop your ear and instincts. These ideas are outlined in *The Practice of Practice* by Jonathan Harnum, which I recommend reading.

Additionally, if you plan to perform or play music in front of other people, there will likely be many emotional hurdles. For this, I recommend *Effortless Mastery* by Kenny Werner. Almost every performer I know struggles with some form of anxiety, and this book has helped most of them, myself included.

I also recommend listening to the type of music you are interested in playing. This seems like strange advice but I'm always a little surprised by how many people I meet who are trying to learn bluegrass mandolin but don't really listen to bluegrass. They enjoy it, and enjoy going to jams, but they don't listen to much bluegrass in their spare time. Even though we have books and instructional videos now, most of the music that we play on the mandolin, bluegrass or otherwise, comes from a folk tradition, which makes understanding the lineage of the sound very important to being able to execute that style. In addition, *active* listening is very important and should be just as big a part of your practice routine as actually playing your instrument. What I mean by this is listening to a piece of music and paying attention to what's happening musically, not just the overall product. To practice this, take a piece of ensemble music that you enjoy and, while you're listening to it, try to focus on one instrument the entire time. The musician may only take a 30-second solo or play some fills here and there, but they're playing the whole time, and listening to what they're doing in the background will help teach you what you should be doing when you're not taking a solo and when you're playing with other people.

Lastly, it's important to remember that making music should be joyful; you should have fun playing the mandolin. It may be frustrating at times but, hopefully, you can enjoy that challenge, as well. I wish you the best of luck and hope to hear you play someday.

ABOUT THE AUTHOR

As the son of a National Banjo Champion, Tristan Scroggins has been surrounded by bluegrass traditions since birth. By age 26, Tristan has been nominated for the International Bluegrass Music Association's Mandolin Player of the Year and for a GRAMMY Award for his participation in the *John Hartford Fiddle Tune Project Vol. 1*.

Tristan has played and taught bluegrass in over a dozen countries and has performed at many prestigious venues, including the Ryman Auditorium and the Grand Ole Opry in Nashville, Tennessee, where he currently resides. With more than a decade of experience as a teacher and workshop instructor, Tristan has gained a reputation for his logically laid out curriculum, generous resources, and relaxed, encouraging presence. Tristan has developed a curriculum that emphasizes inspiration and practice techniques that allow students to overcome their personal musical hurdles.

Made in United States
Orlando, FL
17 April 2022

16921368R00046